John & George
John Dolan

george the Dog

John & George

The Dog Who Changed My Life

John Dolan

CENTURY

Published by Century 2014

2 4 6 8 10 9 7 5 3 1

Copyright © John Dolan 2014

The author has asserted his right under the Copyright, Designs
and Patents Act 1988 to be identified as the author of this work

This book is a work of non-fiction based on the life, experiences and recollections of the author.
In some limited cases names of people, places, dates, sequences or the detail of events have been
changed to protect the privacy of others. The author has stated to the publishers that, except in such
minor respects not affecting the substantial accuracy of the work, the contents of this book are true.

First published in Great Britain in 2014 by
Century
Random House, 20 Vauxhall Bridge Road,
London SW1V 2SA

www.randomhouse.co.uk

Addresses for companies within The Random House Group Limited can be found at:
www.randomhouse.co.uk

The Random House Group Limited Reg. No. 954009

A CIP catalogue record for this book
is available from the British Library

ISBN 9781780892917

The Random House Group Limited supports the Forest Stewardship Council® (FSC®), the leading
international forest-certification organisation. Our books carrying the FSC® label are printed on
FSC®-certified paper. FSC® is the only forest-certification scheme supported by the leading environ-
mental organisations, including Greenpeace. Our paper procurement policy can be found at
www.randomhouse.co.uk/environment

Printed and bound by
CPI Group (UK) Ltd, Croydon, CR0 4YY

Typeset by GroupFMG using Book Cloud

In loving memory of Gerry and Dot Ryan
and Les Roberts

To George the dog

John & George

Prologue

'How much money do you reckon I've made you today, John?' It was Griff, and he was grinning from ear to ear.

'How should I know?' I shrugged. 'A cockle?'

I was sitting on the pavement of Shoreditch High Street, drawing the buildings around me, just as I had done every day for the last three years.

My fingers were freezing cold and I was thinking about whether I could afford to get a cup of tea and a sandwich to keep myself going.

George was next to me, as always, wrapped in a coat and with a paper cup in front of him for passers-by to drop change into.

'How much is a cockle again?'

'A tenner to you, posh boy.'

'No, more than a tenner, John.'

I liked the sound of this. The cup contained just a few pound coins, a handful of silver and a bit of copper, even though we'd been sitting on the street for a good couple of hours. Whatever Griff had made, he'd done better than me and George had that day.

'Hundred quid?' I said, half joking.

'No. Keep going.'

Griff was buzzing. I could feel the energy sparking off him, but I was trying not to let it rub off on me.

'Well, how the hell should I know? Five hundred?'

'Higher.'

'A thousand?'

'Higher.'

I was getting excited now; it was impossible not to.

'Just tell me!'

'John, we're talking thousands.'

'You serious? What d'you mean, thousands?'

'I mean . . . fifteen thousand pounds, to be precise.'

Suddenly I was up on my feet, laughing, frowning and scratching my head in disbelief.

'Straight up? You've made me fifteen thousand pounds? Today? How you done that?'

'I've sold five of your drawings. One alone went for five grand.'

I knew Griff was telling the truth but I couldn't take

it in, not straight away. Good things like this just didn't happen to me.

'You better not be having me on, Griff, because if you are . . .'

'John, it's absolutely true. Five pieces sold. Fifteen grand in total sales.'

George was sitting proud and still as usual, his front legs stretched out before him and his head held high. He began sniffing the air and looking at me expectantly, waiting for my command.

'Come here, George! Come here, boy!'

He sprang onto all fours and pushed his head into my outstretched hands as I crouched down to talk to him.

'Did you hear that, George? Fifteen big ones! I'm gonna be rich.'

I'd been worrying myself to death about losing the roof over my head, but in that split second my fears dissolved. I couldn't believe what I was hearing.

I don't think George could either. He pricked up his ears and tilted his face from side to side, the way he always does when he's listening carefully. His jaw looked set in a satisfied smile and his eyes were shining.

'When do I get my half?' he would have said if he could, because he's a cheeky little git like that. 'Seriously, good on you, mate,' he'd have added, or I'd like to think he would. 'You deserve a break. Just don't forget where your luck came from . . .'

———————

It was spring 2013 when this happened. I was 41 years old and selling those pictures was only the second lucky break I'd had in my entire life.

The first, the really big one, was meeting George a few years earlier. I didn't know it at the time but he was my lucky charm; the dog who would turn my whole world upside down.

Without George I wouldn't have picked up my pen and started drawing again after decades of neglecting my talent, and I would never have met Griff, a.k.a. local art dealer Richard Howard-Griffin. I'd either be lying in the gutter, banged up in jail or buried six feet under, and that's the honest truth.

Instead I've collaborated with some of the world's most famous street artists, my pictures are hanging on walls from New York to Moscow, and I have a sell-out London show under my belt. Getting to where I am now has been one hell of a journey. When I met George I'd been trapped in a revolving door of homelessness, crime, prison, depression and drugs for many, many years.

It was George who finally stopped the door turning, and it was George who made the artist in me stand up and step out of the darkness.

That's no mean feat for a young Staffordshire bull terrier, especially one who'd had a hard life himself before we met. George is my universe. I love him to bits, and this is the story of how he changed my life.

Chapter One

Chapter One

It was the winter of 2009 when George came into my life, and I was living alone in a temporary council bedsit above a newsagent's on Royal Mint Street, down the road from the Tower of London. I'd been fortunate enough to have been there for two years on and off, which was about the only good thing I had going for me. I was struggling in just about every way a person could struggle: I had no job, I had no income, and I had no control over my drug problem. The one thing I did have was the house, and I'd been homeless and slept rough often enough over the years to know how lucky I was to have any kind of roof over my head. As my mum, Dot, had shown me growing up, charity starts at home, and if I met people on the streets less fortunate than myself, I'd sometimes offer to put them up for a night or two. That's how I came to meet Becky and Sam.

I met them outside Tower Hill tube station. They were a nice young couple in their early twenties who were sat begging for change. They, like most other homeless people with their hands out, looked fed up and in need of a break. They had a sheepdog with them who reminded me a bit of a dog I used to look after in my youth, and that's how we first got talking. Over a period of a month or so I got to know Becky and Sam quite well because, as ashamed as I am to admit it, I was begging too; I didn't know what else to do. I used to say to people that I was 'financially embarrassed' but it was much worse than that. I was really struggling to look after myself. I was penniless, and I felt I had no other option but to go cap in hand, asking passers-by if they could spare a bit of change for a hopeless bastard like me. Anyway, whenever I saw Becky and Sam, we'd try to cheer each other up, fetching the odd cup of tea for each other to keep out the cold, or swapping stories about what the punters said to us.

'That fella told me I had a nice smile, gave me a fiver and said I deserved some luck,' Becky would say.

'That geezer told me I was a disgrace to the human race and should throw myself under a double-decker bus,' I'd joke. It wasn't far from the truth, but the only way to deal with it was to laugh it off or you'd just give up.

It was coming up to December and the cold was really starting to set in. I knew from experience what a depressing time that is to be on the streets, so I told Becky and Sam they could stay with me for a while if they wanted. They'd been sleeping rough for two years and unsurprisingly, they jumped at the chance, even though I warned them my bedsit was definitely not the Ritz. It was damp, cold and cramped, with just enough room for my sofa bed, but they were really grateful and happily squashed in, sleeping huddled together with their sheepdog beside them. They told me they'd rescued the dog from a homeless shelter after seeing someone kicking the living daylights out of him, which really got to me. I'd witnessed plenty of acts of senseless abuse and violence over the years, and I'd taken plenty of knocks myself when I'd been down.

'You've done a really good thing,' I said to Becky. 'That's what life's all about.'

A couple of days into their stay, Becky ran up the stairs to the flat looking hassled. Breathless, she asked me if it would be ok to bring another dog in. I was slightly taken aback. When you're homeless, it's important you don't take on too much responsibility. It's difficult enough getting through each day just finding the money to feed yourself. How do you cope with two dogs?!

'Why, sweetheart? Is everything all right? What's happened?' I asked.

'Well, it's a bit of a strange story,' she replied, getting her breath back.

It turned out that a drunk Scotsman had staggered up to Becky at the tube station and asked her if she wanted to buy his dog.

'How much d'you want for him?' she'd asked.

'Price of a strong can of lager – that's all, pet,' the Scotsman said.

'Don't be silly!' Becky had told him. 'You can't sell your dog for a can of lager!'

She looked at the dog who was sat peacefully at the Scotsman's side, minding his own business. He was a young, handsome and very alert animal, and it was clearly an insult to swap him for the price of a can of lager, strong or otherwise. Becky didn't think the Scotsman deserved to have the dog if that's all he thought it was worth, and so she emptied her pockets to see how much money she had on her.

'Tell you what, I'll give you £20,' she said. 'Take that, but don't be coming back now, d'you hear me?'

'Aye, pet. Understood,' he'd replied counting his money. 'By the way, his name is George.'

The Scotsman stumbled off, and Becky was left holding George's worn old lead, wondering what she'd done and hoping I wouldn't mind having him in the flat too.

'Why not?' I said after hearing the story. 'It sounds like this fella needs a break too. Go on, bring him in.'

Becky went back downstairs to fetch him. And a couple of minutes later the door opened again, and in walked George. I was immediately surprised by what a lovely-looking dog he was. Dogs of homeless people aren't always that well cared for, and some can look a bit bedraggled and weak, but although he looked a little nervous I could tell how lively he was. There was something very appealing about the dark patch around his left eye and the fact he had one dark ear and one light one. There was a nick in one of his ears, like he'd been in a fight, but there was no denying what a handsome dog he was.

'A can of strong lager?' I said. 'The guy must be fucking nuts!'

I stroked the top of George's head and said 'Hello,' but I didn't make a big fuss of him because I could see he was a bit twitchy and unsettled. I guess it was hardly surprising. It must have been hard enough for him to be in a strange bedsit with new owners, but God knows what sort of life he'd had with the Scotsman.

'How long did the Scottish fella have him?' I asked.

Becky shrugged. 'I haven't got a clue, but I don't think George is very old.'

I agreed. He wasn't a puppy, but he didn't look much older than, say, eighteen months.

George sat very quietly on the floor, watching and listening, his body unbelievably still. He trained his eyes on whoever was speaking and his ears shot up at the slightest noise coming from outside the flat. Even though he was clearly on his guard, he seemed to have a deep calmness about him. To tell the truth, there was something a little bit mesmerising about George. I liked him right from the start.

———————

Make yourself at home.

'Can you look after George for us for a few hours?' Becky asked a couple of days later. 'I wouldn't ask, only it's really important.'

She and Sam had a meeting with a social worker who was trying to get them off the streets, and Becky explained they didn't want to show up with two dogs. I knew their sheepdog went everywhere with them and I was happy to help. George had been as good as gold in the couple of days I'd known him. He hardly ever barked, he kept himself to himself in the flat, and his calming presence really put me at my ease. He was turning out to be a very welcome guest.

'It'll be my pleasure,' I said. 'You're a good boy, ain't you, George?'

He looked at me and bobbed his head. I didn't think I'd have any trouble with him at all. In fact, I didn't think full stop.

Becky and Sam were gone for ages, and I found myself feeding George with the half a tin of Tesco dog food they had left by the kettle, and giving him a bowl of water. It might have been a very long time since I'd looked after a dog, but even I could work out I'd have to take him outside if they didn't get back soon. I waited as long as I could, until it was just beginning to get dark, and then I gave in. I could tell how bored he was, and it didn't feel right to have a young dog like him sat stewing in my tiny flat. George looked excited when I eventually clipped on his lead, and when I opened the front door, he darted off, pulling me down the stairs like a husky with a sledge.

When we reached the street, I got a very tight grip on him and walked him round the block. I was fretting because with my dodgy arthritic ankle, I knew he was strong enough to pull me over, but I tried not to let it worry me. I just wanted to concentrate on how good it felt to be walking a dog again. It must have been around fifteen years since the last time I had. In fact, it seemed like the first time in fifteen years I'd walked anywhere with a good, honest purpose.

As we meandered through the park, I remembered back to when I was a kid, walking my childhood dog Butch, a beautiful black mongrel, all around the streets of London, wondering what lay ahead for me. What a bloody long time ago that was, and what a massive disappointment my life had turned out to be.

'Life don't always turn out how you expect, does it, mate?' I said to George, who suddenly turned around and licked my hand.

'Oi, behave!' I said. 'What you playing at?'

He nuzzled my leg and it instantly cheered me up. It was like he was trying to say thank you for the walk, and for looking after him. He needn't have. He was the reason

I was outside, taking a walk, breathing in the fresh air rather than being stuck in my miserable little flat, thinking about ways to forget my situation. As much as he owed me, I owed him.

Still, walking George was a bit unnerving because I wasn't used to having any sort of responsibility at all, and it had been a hell of a long time since I'd looked after a dog. As we were walking out of the park, George tipped his head on one side and looked at me intently, as if he was really trying to work me out. I felt like I had to say something to him, to answer the questions in his eyes.

'You'll be all right with me, son,' I told him. 'You have a lie down. Don't you worry about a thing.'

He wrinkled his brow and gave me a withering look. I sat down on a street bench, George lying at my feet, and picked up an old copy of the *Evening Standard* and started flicking through the pages. There was a story about benefit cuts that caught my eye, and I began reading it. One of the many reasons I was in such a state was because my benefits had been cut. It certainly wasn't the whole story – I carried my fair share of the blame – but it was definitely part of the reason why I had ended up begging on the streets, even though that was the very last thing I wanted to do. I desperately needed a break, but with my track record and all the complications I had in my life, nobody in their right mind would have given me a job. I couldn't see any way out of the black hole I had dug for myself; I'd resigned myself to the fact that my life was never going to get any better. It was most likely going to get a lot worse.

As I was reading the story, George sat up between my legs and stuck his nose in the newspaper. 'Cheeky bastard,' I muttered as I pulled the paper away, and roughly started rubbing his head, which he seemed to enjoy, and for the first time I had a good long look at him. I looked deep into his eyes, and he stared right back, unblinking and proud. There seemed to be a connection there between us. There was a great depth in those eyes, an underlying ease, and I remember a feeling of calmness wash over me as we shared that moment. It was the first time in a long time I'd felt anything akin to peace.

———————

Becky and Sam were buzzing when they got back to the flat later that afternoon, and I could see straight away that they were desperate to tell me something.

'Is it good news?' I asked.

They were obviously ecstatic about something, but when she started to speak, Becky sounded a bit nervous.

'The thing is, John. Well, it's like this. We've been offered a flat, but . . .' She looked at George, who appeared to be hanging on her every word.

'That's fantastic!' I interrupted. 'Congratulations! Well done to the pair of you.'

'There's just one problem.'

'Go on . . .'

'We can only take one dog.'

I looked over at George, who was sat quietly, staring down at the floor. God, I felt sorry for him. I knew exactly how it felt to be the one who wasn't chosen, the one who got left behind. I knew there was no way Becky and Sam could turn down the chance of a roof over their heads after sleeping rough for so long. Of course their sheepdog would go with them. George would be the one left without a home.

'Never mind, mate,' I said, walking over and ruffing George's head. 'Handsome bloke like you, you'll find a new home no trouble.'

'Er,' Beckly blurted, and started rubbing her hands together nervously, 'John, I've got something else to ask.'

'What's that?'

'Well, we were hoping you could look after him. What do you think?'

I stared down at George, thought back to our afternoon in the park and knew there was only one answer.

'Course. He can stay with me for as long as you like until you find him a good home. I'd be glad to have the company for a little while.'

Becky smiled but I could tell that she was wasn't quite finished. 'Er, I don't mean just in the short term . . .' she continued, her eyes flitting between George and me. 'I mean, do you want to keep him? Will you take George on?'

I couldn't believe what I was hearing. I hadn't been trusted with anything by anybody for as long as I could remember, and here was Becky offering to give me this beautiful creature.

'Me? You want me to have him?' I said more to myself than to Becky.

'Yes . . . that's if you want him. We've seen how you've looked after him. You're a genuine guy, John. Me and Sam have seen that. We know you'd take good care of him, or we wouldn't ask.'

When you beg for a living, it's not often that you get many compliments, so I was really touched by what Becky was saying. She could obviously tell how well me and George were getting on, which gave me the confidence I needed to say what I said next.

'Really? Well, when you put it like that – flattery will get you everywhere, sweetheart!'

And just like that, it was decided. I slapped my hands on my thighs. 'Come here, George! Come on, boy.'

He picked himself off the floor and trotted over, wagging his tail.

'What did I tell you? Life don't always turn out how you expect, does it, mate?'

Becky and Sam moved out that night and it was very late when I went to bed. In those days I wasn't sleeping well at all, but after making up my sofa bed and settling George down on the floor I fell into a deep sleep really easily. The next morning I opened my eyes to see George lying in the crook of my leg as I lay on my side. I thought I was imagining things for a second. He looked completely relaxed, curled up as if he'd always been there. It took me a minute or two to properly wake up, and when I did my very first thought was: 'What the hell have I gone and done?'

All the confidence I'd had the day before was gone. I was a wreck. No job, no money, no direction. I couldn't even look after myself, let alone George. He was a big dog for God's sake. This was total and utter madness; I would never be able to cope. I closed my eyes, trying to shut out the problem. I hated mornings and was never fit for anything before midday. Normally, from the moment I woke up, I'd start thinking about how I was going to get through the day, or if I'd even survive it at all. I was living on the edge already and having to worry about a dog was the kind of thing that could tip me over. Becky would understand, and if I had to find a new home for George myself, I would.

George stirred and pushed his face right up to mine, making me blink my eyes open again. He was inches away from me, eyeballing me. The flat was freezing cold and he was panting warm clouds of white breath in my face.

'What do you want?' I asked. 'What you doing, eh?'

His brown eyes were shining. He looked alert and excited – the complete opposite of how I was feeling.

'Go on, beat it! I'll be up in a minute. Beat it!'

I picked up my mobile and rang Jackie, my sister. She was the only member of my family I still spoke to, though we could go for six or nine months at a time without talking, and I hadn't seen her in a few years.

'What's up, John?' she asked, because she knew from experience that whenever I called I either had a problem or needed a favour.

'I've done something stupid.'

'You don't say. What is it this time?'

As always, there was a note of sympathy and concern in her voice, even though she must have been bored stiff of dealing with her good-for-nothing little brother.

'I've got a dog, and I can't even look after meself!'

Jackie laughed. 'Are you serious?'

'It's no joke. What am I gonna do?'

'Well, I can think of worse things you could have gone and done. What's the dog called?'

'George.'

He had gone for a nose about, but when I said his name, George came padding back over to me, an expectant look on his face. I realised he probably needed to go outside. All I needed was more sleep, more time to get my head straight and work out my next move.

'What's he like?'

'Beautiful,' I said without thinking. 'He's the most beautiful dog you've ever seen, Jack.' George was now jumping back up on the bed, nudging me and licking my face. 'Look, I'll have to go. The dog's all over me. I'll talk to you later.'

'Ok, I get it,' I said to George, pulling him off me. 'I know you want to go out. Well, if that's what you want, that's what we'll do, while we decide what to do next...'

I had no idea at the time, but right then and there I made a decision that would ultimately change the course of my life. I was going to get out of bed in the morning, not the afternoon, and I was going to take George for a walk because it was what he needed even though it was the very last thing I felt like doing.

It was about half-ten when we headed out together to a small park nearby. Even though it was a bitterly cold day the winter sun was low and shining brightly. My head felt thick and heavy and my eyes were stinging painfully. I couldn't remember the last time I'd been out of the flat so early in the morning. A young mum with a pushchair saw us walking along the pavement and gave us a wide berth. I wondered if she was frightened of dogs like George, but then I realised it was probably me who looked the scarier of the two of us. I had a habit of sleeping in my clothes because the flat was so cold, and I hated washing and shaving because I had no hot water, which made the experience really uncomfortable. I'd lost a few teeth over the years too, which didn't help my appearance. I hadn't looked in a mirror for a long time because I hated the sight of myself so much. On top of all that, I wasn't exactly smelling of roses, and nor was George. I couldn't blame the mum for getting out of our way. The state I was in, I probably wasn't fit to be out in public, and I certainly didn't look capable of being in charge of a dog like George.

Just like the day before, George was pulling hard on his lead, and by the time we got to the park I was really struggling to stay upright. My right ankle was feeling worse than usual and I should have been using my crutches to help me walk, as I often did when my arthritis got really bad during the winter months. But I'd left them back at the bedsit, because I didn't fancy my chances of holding onto George as well as the sticks. That was a battle he was bound to win.

George taking me for a walk.

I'd found an old tennis ball in the flat and had brought it with me to the park. I let George off the lead and threw the ball as far as I could, hoping to give myself a bit of a breather from being dragged around.

He bounded off to fetch it and was back just seconds later with saliva dripping from his jaw and the ball locked firmly in his mouth.

'Good boy! Drop the ball. Drop the ball, George!'

With Butch, the dog I had growing up, that's all I ever needed to say. 'Drop!' was a command he had learned early on and understood very easily, and he obeyed every time. George wasn't having any of it though. He refused to relax his jaw, just sat there clamping down like his life depended on it. Nervously, I reached forward and began

23

to prize the ball out of his mouth with my bare hands. That was the first time I ever tried to reach into George's mouth, and the last. He nearly took my fingers off!

'Oi! Watch it!' I said to George, snatching my fingers out of his mouth. 'I need them.'

He looked at me and seemed to roll his eyes, as if to say: 'You don't say.' I'd started to notice that he always looked me in the eye when I spoke, and I was beginning to see that there was a cheeky streak to his character. I threw the ball again, and this time I had even more trouble getting it out of his mouth. He was snarling and salivating, obviously enjoying the push and shove, and just when I thought I had a good grip on the ball George growled and clamped his teeth even tighter around it. I only just escaped without a nasty bite. That's when it hit me.

'Bloody hell, he's a fully grown animal!' Those were the words that rang through my head. This was serious. If I couldn't even get myself in order, I sure as hell couldn't cope with a muscle-bound pet. I had absolutely no experience with Staffies, or any other similar breed of dog. All I knew was how to look after my old dog Butch, an ordinary mongrel, and that felt like several lifetimes ago.

It would be madness to keep George, utter madness. But then again, I wasn't exactly sane – not back then I wasn't, anyhow.

Chapter Two

Before George walked into my flat and my life started to change, I was a different man. I had been running away from my past for so long that I had almost forgotten where I had come from. I was brought up in a council flat in President House on the King Square estate in Islington, one of many flats in a cluster of low-rise buildings. We were on the third of five floors, and if I stood on the armchair and looked out of the window, as I often did as a small boy, I could see the dome of St Paul's Cathedral, the three towers of the Barbican, and the BP Building in the City of London.

Back in those days I wasn't interested in the buildings – certainly not in the way I am today – I was more concerned with watching out for my dad, Gerry, coming home from work. Gerry was a dustman. He was up at four every morning, out before five and worked until noon, collecting bins in

Camden. He always came straight home to get changed and would then go out to the Bull pub in King Square, where he'd spend three or four hours drinking Guinness before coming home again and sinking into his old Parker Knoll armchair. Supposedly he drank at least twelve pints a day, but when he got home he never looked drunk to me.

'I'm not watching this shit!' he'd always say, changing the TV channel the minute he walked in, regardless of what I was watching. I soon caught on to his routine, and when I heard his key in the door I'd quickly jump up and switch from BBC1 to ITV or vice versa, knowing he would turn back over and I'd end up watching my choice of show anyway. I was always very careful not to get caught because my dad, like most men of his generation, ruled the roost. If he lost his temper his voice would fill the whole flat, the booming sound echoing all around like a pantomime baddie. It put the fear of God in me.

'My house, my rules,' I'd often hear Gerry say. 'If you don't like it, you know where the street door is.' The street door was what we called our front door, even though it was three flights of stairs away from the street. He was a strong, proud man with firm opinions on most subjects. The joke in the family was that if he didn't have a view on a person or a topic, they either hadn't been born yet or it hadn't been invented.

A Simple Drawing of the King Sq Est.
Islington. London. where i grew up!

Like any son, I looked up to my dad and admired him. He loved to read books about the war and he would often tell me stories about battles and soldiers. He was also a gifted artist and could paint anything in any medium, if he put his mind to it. His speciality was sketching portraits, and I remember him once telling me that he drew a portrait of the queen which captured her likeness so well that everyone told him he should send it over to Buckingham Palace. In the end, though, he gave it away to a mate who said he liked it. Gerry was like that – always humble and very generous with his friends. In fact, if there was a party for the locals it was usually in our flat, and if there was a bloke in the pub who didn't have a bed for the night my dad was often the one who stepped in to help.

'Who's that asleep on the sofa?' my mum, Dot, would ask the next morning.

'Last bloke in the pub,' my dad would reply.

She understood Gerry and never complained; my mum had a huge heart and wasn't afraid to roll up her sleeves and help anybody out.

Throughout my childhood she was a cleaner, working every day in offices in the City. She would start early in the morning, before the offices opened, which meant I would go to a neighbour's flat along the landing from six until ten, when she returned.

Dot would go back out again in the evening, to clean after the office workers had left, and stay until seven or eight at night before getting the bus home.

She rarely grumbled but the long days and the physical strain must have been tough at times. There wasn't a huge amount of money around and there were five kids to take care of in the family. She had no choice – we needed every penny.

I was the youngest, and I had two much older brothers, Malcolm and David, who were Dot's sons from a previous relationship. Malcolm was fifteen when I was born and David was seventeen and, from as far back as I can remember, they were both as hard as nails. Malcolm became a professional boxer, and David took over the ownership of the renowned Times Amateur Boxing Club in the early eighties. It was, and still is, at the centre of the community providing young people from every back-ground with an opportunity to participate in sport. David also turned it into an Olympic-standard training facility.

My two sisters, Marilyn and Jackie, were younger than my brothers but still a lot older than me. Marilyn was sixteen when I was born, and was Gerry's daughter from his previous marriage. I barely remember Marilyn being around as she spent a lot of time at her mother's. In fact, I didn't really see her as a sister at all, and I used to call her 'Auntie Marilyn' whenever she showed up, which wasn't that often. My other sister, Jackie, was eight years older than me, and I loved her to bits. My first clear memory of her is when she had to go into hospital to have her tonsils out. I was only about four and I cuddled her as tight as I could and didn't want to let go of her.

She adored our mum and dad and was always well-behaved and kind, helping them out at home and doing her best at school. She used to babysit me, and I thought everything about her was fantastic.

I can't ever remember all five kids living under the same roof; I suppose with seventeen years between me and my oldest brother, and the fact Marilyn stayed with her mother a lot, we were rarely all together. At weekends and after school Jackie would be off with her mates, while I would spend time with my mum and dad, or on my own. As the baby of the family, Gerry and Dot spoilt me rotten. My dad in particular liked to treat me to a comic book from the newsagent when he was on his way home from the pub. At Christmas and birthdays Gerry would take me to Beatties toy shop on High Holborn and sit me on the windowsill outside, so I could press my nose up against the glass.

'Cor, Dad, can I have that *Doctor Who* Tardis?' I'd shout at him in excitement, looking at the shiny blue toy on the shelf.

'Yes, my son, I'll get it for ya.' Gerry would say. His response was always 'Yes, my son', never 'No, we can't afford it.' No matter what our situation was, everything I wanted, I had to have. Once he got me a remote-controlled tank that cost £100 – a hell of a lot of money back then. I always marvelled at the way he would walk into the shop slowly and quietly ask if he could have the toy out of the window.

'Look, John, I got you the exact one you picked out,' he'd tell me outside. Even back then I knew that the battered, faded box the toy came in probably meant he got a bit of a discount. Regardless, every toy he bought was special to me.

As the youngest, I was always able to entertain Dot and Gerry with my antics. They were very liberal and allowed me to express myself. Often, on her way to the local supermarket, Dot would take me to the park on the estate where a load of old dears would be sat on the benches, enjoying the sunshine. She'd settle in next to them and would then get one of the girls to ask me where my old man was.

'At home, drinking!' I'd say, as if I was one of the old ladies and Gerry was my husband.

'What's he like, your old man?' another would ask.

'He's an old bastard,' I'd reply with a cheeky grin. I'd done this routine before and it always brought a chuckle. It was probably the highlight of their day, to hear a young boy like me swearing like a docker.

The more they laughed at my bad language the more I'd spout, until Dot dragged me away. As we walked away we could hear their laughter in our wake; it cracked Dot up too, and even though she told me she disapproved I knew she quite liked it. That's just what they were like; they didn't mind as long as I didn't overstep the mark.

It wasn't long before I was swearing so frequently it became second nature, and I didn't even know I was doing it. Nowadays, I often call to George: 'Come here, you baaaaastard!' when I want him to keep up with me on the street. I say it with affection and it's all a bit tongue-in-cheek. He usually gives me a bored look, as if to say: 'Is there any need for that?' And he'd have a point. But when you've been swearing like I have for my whole life it becomes ingrained in your character.

On Saturdays I'd go up to Chapel Market near Angel with Mum and Jackie. It's the market that features in *Only Fools and Horses,* and it was always bustling with life and characters just as it does on television. We'd always do the same thing: Mum and Jackie would go into Marks & Spencer, then Boots, before going round all the stalls in the marketplace. At the end, we'd have pie and mash from Manze's, the best pie-and-mash shop in London. One particular day, when I was about five years old, I started asking for pie and mash the minute we stepped off the bus.

'Mum, Mum, Mum, I want pie and mash.'

'Not yet, John,'

'I want pie and mash now!'

'Alright, John, we'll get you some in a bit. Just be patient . . .'

I was getting louder and louder and Jackie, who was about thirteen at the time, was dying of embarrassment.

'MUM! I want effin' pie and mash!' I shouted, getting louder still.

I was getting hysterical, and I pulled on Dot's sleeve, refusing to take another step.

'Listen to me, you old cow! I want effin' pie and mash NOW!'

I was stamping my feet and going absolutely mental, and half the market was turning round and staring at me.

My mum looked around and whispered to Jackie: 'Just pretend he's not with us, Jack. Let's just drop him off at the pie and mash shop. Then we'll go and get him later.'

A little old lady saw the state of me and walked over to me. 'What's up, dear?' she asked, giving my mum one of those looks.

'Piss off and mind your own business,' I replied, at which point my mum burst out laughing and steered me straight to the pie and mash shop as fast as she could: it was clear nothing else was going to stop me screaming and making a holy show of her and Jackie.

Sundays were for visiting Nanny Ryan, Gerry's mother. She lived in Shoreditch, not far from where I live now, and she had a mynah bird in a cage called Jack who had a funny habit of mimicking her old friends, as well as relatives who had died. Nanny Ryan would give me 50p and after an hour-long visit I'd say goodbye and off I'd go to the Brick Lane Sunday flea market, down Bethnal Green Road. It was well known for selling electrical goods that never worked; you'd be lucky you didn't electrocute yourself or blow your house up with some of the gear down there. My nan's friend bought a songbird there once, only to find the bottom part of its beak was missing and it couldn't utter a note; she was given this disappointing news when she took it to the vet to find out what was wrong.

Stories like that were ten a penny; it was par for the course to pay your money and take your chances in a market like that – but it didn't stop people flocking there, enjoying the buzz and hoping to find a bargain. It was always packed, and I can remember seeing skinheads in their Crombies and Doc Martens, selling National Front newspapers at the junction of Brick Lane and Bethnal Green Road, with a cordon of police standing in front of them.

I loved the place, mainly because I'd always have an apple fritter and then go to Sclater Street to buy second-hand comics. I'd choose the old American Marvel and DC comics – Batman and Superman and some others – but all I was interested in as a kid was copying the pictures.

When we got back from the market I'd sit in my bedroom for hours with a pencil and a bit of paper, trying to copy the characters, to capture the bold lines of their facial expressions and the movement in their muscles. The shading was particularly important to me and I would focus on it in minute detail, balancing the greys in my drawing and making sure the picture I composed was as close to the one from the comic as possible. If I made a mistake, I wouldn't bother rubbing it out, I'd just start a new drawing, and after a couple of hours my bedroom would be strewn with scrunched-up pieces of paper. I couldn't stop until I'd captured every tiny detail of the drawings and managed to figure out the techniques the artists used. When I was drawing, nothing in the world could bother me.

Chapter Three

When I was still only about five years old, Jackie started to go out with my mum in the evenings, helping her to clean offices on Fleet Street and Tottenham Court Road. That left me and my dad home alone together, and nine times out of ten he'd fall asleep in his armchair. I'd usually have a look through my comics, draw a few pictures or watch a bit of TV, but Gerry would be out cold for ages, having sunk a few pints in the afternoon, and after a while I'd start to get bored.

The flat wasn't a very interesting place for a small boy on his own. To pass the time when I wasn't drawing, I used to look at myself in every one of the mirrored tiles around the fireplace and study all the dials on the big mahogany pendulum clock that Dot had bought from a catalogue and put above the mantelpiece. But that only kept me interested for so long; and with so much happening right outside the front door, my curiosity got the better of me.

One evening I decided to go out for a little walk. To make sure I didn't wake Gerry up, I propped cushions over his ears, and then I pulled a chair up to the street door, slid the lock across, and nipped out as quietly as I could.

I wandered back and forth along the passageway outside our house for a while until I plucked up the courage to go a little further and headed down the communal stairwell. As it happened, a boy called David, who lived in Turnpike House and was a little older than me, had also given his old man the slip that evening. I bumped into him outside the bin chute a couple of floors down from our flat. We both smiled when we caught each other's eye.

'Alright, John!' David said too loudly, and then, a little shiftily asked me if I fancied going to the underground car park.

'That's a good idea,' I answered, keeping my voice to a whisper, and we scampered off down the stairs together, punching each other's arms and giggling under our breath.

The car park was for the residents of the estate but it had many other uses. Teenage boys would take their girlfriends down there for a quick tongue pie and a knee trembler, while glue sniffers loitered in the dark corners, grunting to each other like a bunch of orang-utans because they were so off their nuts they could no longer speak. The police knew about the car park and they would turn up all the time, at which point the glue sniffers would run in all directions, with one or more invariably getting caught and dragged home to be shamed in front of their parents, empty crisp bags stinking of glue presented as evidence.

Students from nearby City University used to raid the car park at the end of term, stealing cars to get themselves home for the holidays. Residents from our estate would often turn up looking for their car, only to find an oil stain on the ground where it had been parked the day before.

On this particular night, when me and David got down to the car park, he went straight over to a row of gleaming cars and started eyeing up a beautiful red Ford Cortina with a chrome finish. I didn't know it yet, but David had it in mind to set it alight. Don't ask me why – looking back I can't for the life of me remember – but when David pulled out a box of matches, gave me a look, and told me to gather up some old newspapers and rubbish from the bins, I didn't argue with him. I thought it would be a laugh. I guess we were just too young or too stupid to consider what the end result would be.

Together, we started stuffing all the newspapers and rubbish under the Cortina, then we stepped back and David whispered: 'Let's burn it!' I struck a match and put it to the paper. Nothing happened at first, so I struck a few more and threw them under the car. And just then, as the small flames began to flicker into life, a police car pulled up and two huge coppers got out.

'Oi, you two!' one of them said. 'What are you playing at! Did you light that fire?'

David and I both froze on the spot. I'd never been in serious trouble before, and even though I was used to seeing the police around the estate, I never thought I'd be the one they were after. I was absolutely terrified. Before we knew it, the policemen had put out the flames and bundled us into the back of their panda car.

'We're taking you home,' they told us, and as we headed for the exit David pointed out that they didn't have to drive out of the estate as our flats were right above the car park. He had that much more confidence than me, and didn't look nearly as afraid. I was sat there, eyes tight shut, thinking about everything my parents would say and do. In fact, right then David started giggling in the back of the car.

'What you laughing at?' one of the policemen demanded, flicking his head round and looking at David.

'Him,' David laughed, pointing at me. 'He's crapped his pants.'

'Oh, he ain't, has he?' the copper said, leaning in towards me and having a sniff.

'Oh, bleeding hell, he has. Serves him right!'

The next thing I knew, I was in the lift at President House, feeling like I was being taken to prison rather than back to my home.

Gerry was furious to be woken up by two policemen knocking on the door. I shouldn't even have been out at that time of the evening, let alone attempting to set fire to a car. To cap it all, I was stinking and shaking.

'You little baaaastard!' Gerry growled at me when the 'filth', as he called the police, had left. 'Wait till your mother hears about this, you little baaaastard.' He took me into the bathroom and started scrubbing me hard with our bathroom brush, all the while shouting and cursing at me. I was hoping that I'd get a fairer hearing from my mum, but when she came home later that evening and Gerry told her what I'd done, she gave me a good clip round the ear.

I didn't hear the end of it for at least a week. The shouting and swearing would last all day until the moment I went to bed, and would start again as soon as I got up the next morning. When I was locked in my bedroom drawing, I would overhear Gerry and Dot complaining to Malcolm, David and Jackie that I was becoming a little brat. My brothers and sister stood up for me, as they always did, but sadly it wasn't long before I was letting them down all over again.

One evening a week or so after my first run-in with the law, I was bored stiff and fancied another little walk around the flats. I thought if I didn't go far and do anything stupid like last time, I'd be alright. Gerry had sunk a few pints of cider when he got home from the pub, and was out like a light, snoring his head off louder than usual. I tiptoed past him, squeaked open the door, leaving it on the latch so I could get back in later, and escaped along the balcony. I was strolling aimlessly around the corridors and stairwells for a bit, wondering what to do next, when I bumped into two older boys, Terry and Derek. They must have been around thirteen or fourteen, were wearing ripped T-shirts like the punks did back then, and had a real swagger about them. I was definitely in awe of them.

'What you doing out this time of night, John?' Terry asked me.

'My dad's out cold on the booze,' I said, feeling really grown-up. 'I'm just having a little walk, that's all. I've left the door on the latch.'

They looked at each other quickly. 'Well then, we best get you home, ain't we?' Derek said, insisting on walking me back to the flat. That scared me. I was worried, after the last time, that Gerry would go spare if he knew I'd been wandering around the flats again.

'Don't tell the old bastard what I've been up to, will you?' I said.

'Nah, course not, John. We'll just see you inside safe and sound, don't you worry.'

They pushed open our street door and came right into the flat with me. Gerry was still out cold, but instead of just dropping me off and leaving me there, one of them started searching through the drinks cabinet in the living room, pocketing a bottle of Gordon's gin, while the other one knelt down beside Gerry and sneakily lifted his wallet out of his trouser pocket. I just stood in the corner silently and watched them, unable to do a thing. I so wanted to shout and wake Gerry up to tell him what was happening, but I knew that would give me away.

They couldn't have been there for more than a couple of minutes, but just as they were about to leave, one of them bumped into the dresser, which made the glasses inside chink together. Right then, Gerry woke up. He opened his eyes, saw the two boys and bolted straight up out of his chair, grabbing for the one nearest him. He caught Terry by his sleeve, just enough to hold him in place while Derek managed to scamper away, not looking back. Once he had Terry in his grasp, he didn't even speak – he just looked him up and down and gave him a good, hard slap across the jaw, then told him to fuck off. I heard on the grapevine that a few days later my brother Malcolm had found Derek and had given him the same treatment. There was no comeback from Terry and Derek's parents – that was how kids were treated back then. You did something wrong, you took your punishment and you didn't complain.

Of course, I was in the doghouse again, good and proper, but this time at least the heat wasn't all on me, because the two older lads were in far more trouble than I was. Nevertheless, Gerry wouldn't let up and shouted at me all night, telling me what an idiot I was for hanging out with such scumbags. I tried to explain that it wasn't like that, but he was having none of it. Looking back, I could see a change in how Gerry looked at me from that point forward. Even though I was still very young, I guess he decided that I wasn't ever to be totally trusted again.

I started at Morland Primary School around this time. It was opposite the Gordon's Gin factory on Goswell Road and just across the street from our flat. If Dot was washing up at the kitchen sink she could see straight into the playground, which would later turn out to be a mixed blessing. I was a very chubby kid, thanks to all the crisps and sweets I was allowed to help myself to, and the fact that I spent a lot of my time indoors, shut away in my bedroom drawing, or lounging in front of the TV. I'd never really noticed it before, but my weight suddenly started to become a real problem once I was at school. My mum and Jackie were both slim, but Gerry was a thick-set man and a few other members of my family were what you might charitably call 'well built'. I'd always been on the big side, but at home I had never worried about my size, or felt like the odd one out. Now, it was different. Compared to all the normal-sized five- and six-year-olds in my class I was huge, and I started to feel self-conscious about my weight. Coming home from school, I would ask my mum whether she thought I was fat, but she would just laugh it off and with a hint of pride tell me that I was a 'growing boy'.

The kids at school soon had other ways of describing me. I became known as 'the fat kid', Billy Bunter or Fatty Arbuckle – whichever fat cartoon or comic character they'd heard of. Giant Haystacks and Big Daddy were others names thrown at me, which would fizz around my mind whenever I watched the wrestling on Saturday mornings.

The bullying quickly became relentless, and I grew to hate school because of it. Games lessons were always an ordeal because I suffered from asthma too. I'd be out of breath after two minutes' exercise, coughing my guts up like an old geezer on forty fags a day. Even though it was really getting to me, I didn't tell anyone at school or at home how bad the bullying was. In the seventies you didn't have all this counselling and pastoral care you have nowadays – you just got on with it.

Dot could obviously see how big I was and knew I had worries about my size, but she still didn't stop me eating whatever I wanted whenever I wanted it. She'd always let me have 10p for an afternoon snack of a packet of chips or a bag of sweets, even after I'd eaten a huge plateful of chops and mash and a handful of custard creams for lunch.

I think one of the reasons for this was that my mum and dad were both war babies, born within a few months of each other in 1939. They remembered the days of rationing and, like lots of people of their generation, they thought it was kind to give their kids treats whenever they could. Nobody went on diets in their day, and I reckon Dot thought my puppy fat would fall off me naturally as I got older and taller.

'Don't worry, he's only a kid – he'll grow out of it' was a phrase I heard an awful lot at that age. It's what parents told each other all the time on our estate. It's a pity it wasn't always true.

———————

Away from school, I was spending more and more time exploring the estate. The characters and goings-on around

Turnpike House fascinated me, and it was always an education to walk around King Square park and the streets surrounding the flats. Back then, parents let their kids off the leash much more. There wasn't the same concern as there is now of kids running into strangers; we tended just to laugh at their weirdness, rather than be freaked out by it, and there were plenty of characters to offer up entertainment.

If you went out in the early evening, the chances were you'd see old Nelly falling out of the pub, singing war ballads and music hall favourites at the top of her voice. Nelly was an aging spinster who didn't like men, but did love a drink. 'It's a long way to Tipperary . . .' she'd bellow. 'It's a long way to go . . .'

Then, all of a sudden, her singing would be drowned out by the noise of breaking glass as one of the flat's residents would throw wine bottles at her from their balcony. 'Oi, pipe down will ya! Take that!' you'd hear, followed by a loud SMASH. For some reason the bottles were usually filled with colourful bath crystals, and miraculously Nelly always seemed to dodge them without ever missing a beat.

'Goodbye, Piccadilly, farewell, Leicester Square . . .'
SMASH!
'It's a long, long way to Tipperary . . .'
SMASH!
'But my heart's right THERE!'

SMASH! SMASH! SMASH!

Old Joe Curran was also part of the landscape. He was an elderly Jewish gent who told everyone he served as a seaman in a famous World War II battle, though he never said which one. He rode around on a really smart pushbike, and sometimes, usually in the days leading up to an election, you could find old Joe out on the main drag of Goswell Road with a loudspeaker and a political poster shouting out slogans.

'Vote Labour!' he'd cry one week. The next it would be: 'Support the National Front!' or 'Margaret Thatcher for prime minister!'

He would also make random references to whatever was going on in the country at the time. I can remember him banging on about the riots at the Notting Hill Carnival in one breath and then Harold Wilson's resignation in the next, as if they were part of the same story. I was never sure if they were or not, but from the funny looks all the older people gave him I don't think he ever made much sense.

Old Joe was notorious for other things too. He'd raid dustbins, then bend your ear off about the marvellous things he'd found. It might be a Sex Pistols record that had a scratch he reckoned he could fix, or it could be a broken kitchen blender he was going to use the parts of to mend half a dozen other things.

Old Nelly having a sing-song as the bottles rained down.

Joe had a succession of dogs and raved about each one he owned. God knows where he found them – they were most likely strays and always young mongrels – but when they reached a certain age and he'd had enough of them he got rid of them, as if they were useless bits of junk he'd found in the bins. He would take the dog on a bus or a train to Wanstead, right out in East London, let it off the lead and leave it there. Why Wanstead, I don't know – all I knew was that it was about twenty-five miles away and he hoped the dog wouldn't find its way home. If by some miracle the poor dog did find its way back to our estate, the rumour among us kids was that old Joe would kill it. Horrible really, when I look back on it now. I always liked the dogs that you saw around the estate, and Joe Curran's story bothered me no end. I could never get my head around what he did, especially as he seemed like such a harmless old boy the rest of the time.

I became very fond of a black Alsatian called Max, who was legendary around Islington. I don't know if he had an owner, but you'd always see him running around the estates, up and down the stairwells and through the park, with a string of neighbourhood kids chasing after him. He was such a sparky, beautiful dog but he used to hang around with a scruffy little brown and white mongrel called Whiskey who wasn't quite as popular. Nobody paid him any attention, and some of the big kids would kick him up the rear to chase him off. He was jumpy because of it, and I always felt sorry for him and made sure I gave him a bit of fuss when I could, gathering him up in a big hug and rubbing his head as I do now with George. One day both Max and Whiskey managed to get hit by zooming cars, on a busy road near Old Street, which really upset me when I heard about it. I'd so loved running around with those dogs. I don't know if Gerry felt sorry for me, or just because I wouldn't shut up about it, but it wasn't long after that we got a little black crossbreed mongrel called Butch.

I was nearly ten years old when Butch arrived, and he more or less instantly became *my* dog because I was the one who was always around to walk him and play with him at home. It didn't take long for me to start to train Butch and teach him a few tricks: sitting, heeling and dropping – basic stuff really, but a lot of fun nevertheless. He was a funny dog in every way. For a start he wasn't exactly a 'butch' dog! I think whoever named him was having a good laugh. He was a panicky, delicate little dog, but if you put your clenched fist under his nose he'd show you his teeth and growl. The very best thing about Butch was taking him for walks. On the weekends, or during the school holidays, I used to wake up really early, grab a quick breakfast and spend all morning taking him out around the Square Mile, or all over the Barbican estate, which was still quite new back then. He was a beautiful little dog and people would walk right up to us, give him a pat on his head and pay him compliments. Whenever I was out with Butch I didn't think about anything else except which way we were going to walk next. The bullying at school, the worrying about being fat or the latest trouble I'd been in with my mum and dad went out of my head. The world was my oyster and the streets of London were paved with gold; that's exactly how I felt as a young boy walking my dog.

Chapter Four

When I was young things used to be a lot simpler – happier, if you didn't count going to school. We were undoubtedly poor and living on a massive council estate, but when the sun shone there really wasn't anywhere better. Back then, I used to love it when the local council play lorry would roll up near our flat. Driven by a couple of big old girls, the lorry would park up on the grass in King Square and kids from all the local flats would swarm around it like locusts. The two women would pull the sides down, revealing climbing ropes and plastic shapes carved into the sides of the van, making it look like an oversized baby shape sorter. Next to the van they would erect a big inflatable mattress that you had to take a giant run up to scramble onto. It was the size of two double-decker buses and you had to be a tough kid to get up there and stand your ground, but once you were up on it, you could bounce high up into the sky. We never had any local funfairs come visit us, but we didn't need them; this was our version of a bouncy castle.

Not long after the play lorry would turn up, you could hear the sound of the ice-cream van ringing in the distance. As it got closer, all the kids would jump off the lorry and run to their mums asking for 10p to buy a Rocket or a Fab. Other kids would be peering up to the tower blocks of Turnpike House or President House, shouting up to different windows trying to get their mum's attention.

I was no different, and I once asked my brother David who was sunbathing on the grass for some money for a Mr Whippy.

'Those who ask don't get, and those who don't ask don't want,' was his reply.

I stood there, confused, trying to get my head around what he'd just said. Needless to say, I didn't get an ice cream that day; I just sat there on a bench looking at the other kids tucking into theirs and scratching my head, trying to figure out what he meant.

Other days all us kids would play soldiers. Somebody had a key to the bike sheds on one of the other estates, and we'd break in and pretend one of us was the sergeant major while the other two had to march and follow orders around the shed. We'd also sit and listen to a portable radio, joining in when our favourite songs came on, like 'Video Killed the Radio Star' by the Buggles.

For 60p you could buy a Red Bus Rover ticket in the sweet shop, which you could use on any bus. We'd climb on the back of the old Routemaster double-decker and end up miles away, on our very own tour of London, visiting places like the London Dungeon, HMS *Belfast* and the Royal Festival Hall on the river Thames.

If we had burned through our pocket money we would play Tin-Can Tommy, which was a cross between tag and hide-and-seek. I often struggled to keep up with the other kids, because it didn't take much for me to get out of breath on account of my weight and asthma. Even with all the running around I did back then, I still had rolls of fat around my middle and a double, if not triple, chin. I was pushing thirteen stone by the time I was nine years old, which was alarming considering I was only four foot tall. I didn't help myself though: the more I got bullied at school, the bigger I got, eating my way through crisps, sweets, ice creams and bags of chips, anything I could get my hands on. One day, when I was pretending to be sick to get away from school, I heard a commotion outside and stood at the window of the flat to see what was going on. There was a film crew on the top of Turnpike House, shooting the video for Pink Floyd's

'Another Brick in the Wall'. I sat there and watched them film the whole thing and to me it felt like I was part of that video. I pretended I was the big star on the set of a Hollywood movie. Of course, I've seen the video many times since on TV, and the meaning of it hits me every time. I was one of those kids Roger Waters was singing about: school was the wall for me.

Looking back and seeing how my life has turned out, I guess you could say I wasn't school material. Maths and English were completely alien to me and geography and history just bored the life out of me. The only thing I ever showed any ability in was art. It was the one class I understood without the teacher having to explain over and over. It came very naturally to me and I just seemed to know instinctively how to draw. Obviously, it helped that I'd been copying out my comics for a while, but I still found that drawing shapes and images was something I did without even thinking about it. I used to doodle all the time through the more boring classes, and would always have a pencil or felt tip on the go, squiggling whatever popped into my mind, be it someone's face or a quick portrait of Butch, or something else I'd seen that day that had caught my eye.

During the course of that school year my brother David noticed how much I was struggling with my appearance.

He caught me staring at the mirror squeezing my belly in to make myself look slimmer. He didn't say anything at the time but one day he came to pick me up after school. Before I could say anything he just came out and said it. 'I know about the bullying, John, and I know it must be really hard for you. I'm taking you to my club where you're gonna learn how to box.' He told me that it would help with the bullies, that once they found out I was a boxer, they were less likely to pick on me. I could have cried – I felt so blessed to have my big brother looking out for me.

Still, I can remember walking into the club for the first time and feeling really scared. Everything seemed so vast and stark under the harsh spotlights. The boxing ring was in the middle of the floor, and there were two massive guys slinging punches at each other. The other thing that I remember is the sound: the deep, muffled thuds of the punches landing. David gave me a pair of gym shorts and a vest and put me through a tough warm up where I had to skip, run and do star jumps and sit-ups. I felt so conscious that I was showing him up, with my fat little belly popping out every now and then, but after a while I just got into it and started on a soft punch bag, and then a hard one, and learned how to move my feet. It was hard work and I was puffing and panting, but I stuck at it. David had told me how important the footwork was, and I concentrated really hard, listening to every word the trainer said to me.

'That's it my son, you're dancing with the punches! You're gliding like a butterfly!'

Me as a boy boxing.

It really spurred me on. After going twice a week for a month I was ready for the ring. I'd be paired up with kids who were four or five years older than me, because you had to be matched on weight, not age, and only the teenagers weighed thirteen-odd stone like me! I would hold my own and with each sparring match I felt my confidence grow. Before long I was dreaming of walking into the playground, looking like Sylvester Stallone in *Rocky*, and knocking the living daylights out of every kid who had ever bullied me. Just imagining it was enough to make me feel better. The bullying had gone on for far too long, but I felt like I was finally turning a corner and I was hopeful about the future.

Chapter Five

My days of training at the boxing club and mucking about on the estate are still some of the happiest memories I carry with me. Life had a nice routine to it and I felt that everything was going my way. I was getting quite good at boxing, my footwork was improving, and I noticed that my weight had started to come off. When Dot saw that my clothes didn't fit anymore, she just smiled at me knowingly. She didn't mind taking my school trousers in, even after her long shift cleaning. I guess I was the one who was most surprised by my own transformation. I knew David was proud and he made a big fuss of me. Even Gerry, who was normally the most reserved, had taken to calling me 'champ'.

'Son, I've got something to tell you,' my dad said to me one day.

His voice was like gravel and immediately I knew that this wasn't just another conversation about boxing or my comics or Butch misbehaving in the flat. Nor did I think he was about to tell me off. No – from his tone of voice, this immediately felt much bigger, and the only thing I couldn't guess was how important and life-changing his next words would be.

I'd met him coming out of the pub on my way back home from school, and he'd taken me to the newsagent round the corner, as he sometimes did, to buy me a comic. On these rare occasions we would sit together on our living-room floor and he would pick out the illustration he wanted me to copy. He would never say anything whilst I was drawing. It was enough for him to see that I'd inherited some of his talent for art.

On our way to the newsagent he would normally ask me which comic I was thinking of buying. I was really into the Judge Dredd comics and was ready for the question. This time, however, he was really quiet, letting his 'something to tell you' line linger in the air for a long while.

'What, Dad? What is it? What do you have to tell me?' I said, walking next to him. I couldn't hold it in.

'I'm sorry, son, I made a mistake. You're too young to understand. I'll tell you when you're older,' he said, backtracking.

I was a boxer, a fighter – big enough and old enough to take anything on the chin.

'Come on, Dad! What is it? Can't you tell me now? Please, Dad? This is not fair!'

He shook his head and looked at the ground. 'No, son, when you're older.' He was firmer, more resolute now. 'When you're older,' he repeated, stomping on the words. 'I'll tell you when you're older, OK?'

It wasn't OK, not with me. I badgered him all the way through the estate, up the stairs and along the passageway to our flat.

'Go on, Dad, please! Dad, Dad, Dad, please! Just effin' tell me.'

At that he stopped and turned to look at me. I thought I was in real trouble, but as he put his key in the lock, he gently said: 'Alright, son, I'll tell you.'

———————

I had to wait until we were fully indoors. We shouted hello to my mum in the kitchen as we walked through the living room and into the bedroom. He pushed the door to and asked me to sit beside him on the bed. Then he took off his cap, putting his arm gently around my shoulder, and gave me a tiny squeeze. He never did this. He was never one to show his emotions or give any signs of affection. I could feel my heart beating faster and faster. I tried really hard to steady my breathing because I could tell this wasn't going to be good news at all and I needed to be on my guard. My dad took a very deep breath and delivered the dreaded blow.

'Son, it's like this. You know you call me Dad, and you call your mum Mum? Well, there's no easy way to say this, but we're not your real mum and dad. What I mean is, we're your grandparents. Do you understand what I am trying to say John?'

Time stopped. All I could do was look him in the eye, trying really hard not to blink. I wanted to show I wasn't afraid but I couldn't stop the tears from filling my eyes. I heard my heart thump in my ear. Why was he making this up? What had I done for him to say this? How could he say he wasn't my dad?

'It ain't true,' I said after what seemed like hours. 'You're lying! It can't be true . . . is it Dad?'

'I am afraid it is, John, and I am so sorry you have to find out now, like this. But you don't need to worry about it. It's no different. It don't change nothing. We still love you the same. In fact, we love you more because you are so much more precious to us.'

It hit me hard, all of it, right in the pit of my stomach, and I knew it had to be true.

I was too stunned to ask questions, and it didn't even occur to me to ask or try to work out who my real parents were. I was too concerned with who they weren't.

Gerry carried on talking while I sobbed and spluttered snot all down my school shirt. My shoulders juddered up and down beneath the weight of his arm and I couldn't control myself. I was devastated.

'You know Auntie Marilyn?' I heard him say as I tried to listen to his words.

I nodded. Of course I knew Auntie Marilyn. I didn't see much of her, but she was my sister, wasn't she?

'Well, Auntie Marilyn is your mum,' he said calmly, as if it was the most natural thing.

I was totally distraught, bawling uncontrollably, tears streaming down my cheeks as I tried and failed to keep it together.

'No, it ain't true, Dad. It can't be. You're my dad.'

Marilyn was Gerry's daughter, so she had to be my sister, didn't she? She had to be! I was confused.

'I'm sorry, lad, but it's true. But like I say, it don't change nothing at all. You are and always will by my youngest son.'

A picture of Marilyn came into my head. I could see her round, smiling face, her short, dark hair and her slim, shaped eyebrows. She plucked her eyebrows until they were really thin, because that was the fashion in the early eighties, but I always thought it was such a weird thing to do, to pull your own hair out. Did I look anything like her? I didn't know; I couldn't think straight at all. I could barely remember the last time I'd seen her.

Whoever she was – auntie, sister or mum – I didn't know her, not really. And at this moment in time I didn't care. To me she was someone who drifted in and out of the flat, someone who I was told to call 'Auntie Marilyn'. She didn't show me any special attention or affection, and she wasn't even there on all of my birthdays or at Christmas. Sometimes I didn't even think she noticed I was there at all.

'Do I have to go back?' I gasped the question out, not knowing where 'back' was, because I had never been to Marilyn's house. I knew she'd lived in another part of London with her mum most of the time when I was younger, but I didn't have a clue where she lived now. I was nearly ten, so she must have been about twenty-six. She had a whole life outside our immediate family and I knew nothing about it.

'No, you're happy here. Your mum loves you, but of course you don't have to go back.'

Dot appeared at the door – or maybe she had been standing there all along, I wasn't sure. Her wavy blonde hair was falling around her shoulders, and I remember thinking that she didn't look like a grandmother at all. Dot wasn't old or frail. She had a flowery apron around her waist and was wearing a long, baggy cardigan as usual, but she didn't look like a grandmother; she just looked like a mum. My mum.

'Gerry! What are you doing?'

'He had to be told one day.'

'Yes, I know. But why today? And why not tell him in my company? We haven't talked about this!'

I don't think Gerry himself knew the answers to those questions. All he knew now was that the secret was out. Marilyn was his daughter, and I suppose he felt it was ultimately his responsibility to be the one to tell me the truth. His house, his rules. I carried on crying and Gerry kept his arm around me as he told me more and more.

I can't remember exactly when or in what order I was given more information, but this is what I was eventually told about how I came into the world.

Marilyn was always flitting between Gerry and Dot's and her mother's house, and at some point when she was sixteen years old she ran away – or at least Gerry didn't see her for three months. When she eventually turned up she had a big fat belly and was around seven months pregnant.

Her boyfriend at the time was a guy called Jimmy Dolan. The name rang a bell, and I realised it was a guy I'd seen in the flat quite a few times. I never really knew why he was there, or who he was friends with in the family; he was just a bloke called Jimmy who all the family seemed to know, and from what I could remember they didn't seem to ever make him very welcome. I think I was told to call him 'Uncle Jimmy', but I knew he wasn't my real uncle because he was definitely not welcomed with open arms.

Gerry told me that Marilyn didn't want to settle down with Jimmy, and she was way too young to bring up a baby on her own. They agreed that she would have the baby and give it up for adoption. She gave birth to me in Hackney General, and Gerry made a point of telling me very clearly that Marilyn took one look at me and fell in love with me, even though I was the loudest baby on the ward! 'There was no way you were being given up for adoption, John – no way.'

'That's why me and your mum took you in,' Gerry said. 'None of us wanted to let you go.'

I'd never questioned before why I was the only person in the family with the surname Dolan. That surprises me when I think about it now, although I suppose I was just too young to give it much thought. I guess it was only a matter of time before I started asking awkward questions, and maybe that's what made Gerry speak out when he did.

It was all too much for me to take in. My dad was my granddad. His daughter was my mum. My mum was my nan. And what about Malcolm and David? I thought they were my big brothers. But now? They were what? My uncles? I decided it didn't matter; I wasn't going to think of them as uncles. They would always be big brothers to me, and Jackie would always be my big sister. Nobody was going to take that away from me.

As I recall, everything went straight back to normal immediately after this news came out, because that's how I wanted it to be. I didn't talk about it with anybody, nobody said anything to me, and I tried to forget about it.

'It's no different. It don't change nothing.' That's what Gerry had told me, and I wanted him to be right. If I ever got a strange feeling in my stomach, I would keep repeating those words until I felt better.

I still walked Butch, I still went boxing, I still got bullied at school and I still ate my dinner at the same table and slept in the same bedroom.

'There's my brother!' I'd say proudly if I saw Malcolm or David walking up to President House. 'My sister Jackie's babysitting tonight, because my mum and dad are going out,' I'd tell my mates. Nothing had changed, I was absolutely adamant about that. I overheard Gerry telling Marilyn on the phone one day that he'd told me everything. 'I had to tell him,' Gerry said sternly.

I didn't see Marilyn for about five or six months after that, which wasn't unusual. When she finally did walk into the flat I refused to look at her any differently, and she didn't act any other way. I still called her Auntie Marilyn and she never said anything about the past to me, ever. I was glad about that, but unfortunately there was another upset waiting around the corner.

I don't think it was very long afterwards that Gerry came up to me with the same serious look on his face he'd had on the day he sat me down on the bed and dropped bombshell. My stomach immediately began turning over again.

'Son, there's something else you need to know.'

'What?' I asked nervously. I wanted to put my hands over his mouth to stop the words coming out. Instead I kept my own mouth shut and sat there and listened, scared witless.

'I want to tell you the truth, son,' Gerry said. 'I don't want you listening to no gossip.'

One of the neighbours had been talking, and this next family skeleton was about to fall out the closet very soon. He took a deep breath, put his arm around my shoulder, just like he did that day and told me the latest secret. Jackie, my big sister, was adopted too. I hung on his every word, eyes like saucers as he told me Jackie's story, and in a cruel way, I felt relieved that I wasn't the only one.

Like Gerry said, it didn't matter; it didn't change a thing. I knew the truth now, and it was just another family story to store away and forget about as quickly as possible. To me Jackie was and still is my big sister.

Everything was back to normal – that's what I told myself the next day and the next, until I totally believed that it was.

Chapter Six

It wasn't long after Gerry told me those family secrets that I had the bright idea of playing truant from school. If you had asked me back then why I did it, I'd probably have said: 'I've had enough of the bullying. Can't take no more.' The bullying *was* still really bad, that much was true, but looking back now, I'm sure that learning the truth about my family impacted on me in ways I'm still only beginning to understand. I spent a lot of time denying the truth to myself and even more time running away – and school was the easiest thing to run from. I was still really fat and eating as much as ever, and it seemed like whatever weight I lost at the boxing club I would pile straight back on. I'd go through periods of not going to the club for weeks and I was still overeating every day, so it's hardly surprising I didn't turn into Rocky overnight. The kids at school wouldn't let me forget it either.

Playing truant seemed like the ideal solution: if I wasn't in school and I wasn't getting bullied, all my problems would be solved. No other kids my age bunked off. I think it was quite unheard of for a primary-school kid to play truant, but I had it all worked out. Dot and Gerry were both at work in the day and Jackie was going to college by then. I was old enough to take myself to school, so it was easy enough not to turn up.

I would leave my house in my uniform at ten to nine as usual, making sure I said a proper goodbye to Butch, but instead of walking down the stairs and across the road to school, I would walk up to the top floor of President House. Looking both ways over each shoulder, fancying myself as some sort of shifty character I'd seen on *Starsky and Hutch* or *T. J. Hooker*, I'd dart along the passageway that lead to the roof, knowing that nobody would find me there.

The roof was where the older boys would smoke a crafty joint at night, but in the daytime it was usually deserted. Once I was up there, I'd curl up and put my head on my school bag and go to sleep for as long as I could, or I'd take out my pens and pencils and start sketching away idly as the clouds turned. I did the same thing day after day. If it got cold it wouldn't bother me; it wasn't school, and that was all that mattered to me. The problem was, as much as I loved not being in school and being alone up on that roof, I couldn't stave off the boredom, and so I began looking for things to keep me occupied.

I'd noticed that the milkman always made his deliveries around nine-thirty every morning, and that he'd leave at least one bottle of milk outside every doorway. One day, after spending an hour or so lounging up on the roof, I walked back down and began picking up every bottle and chucking it over the side of the building. I didn't look where the bottles were landing but I could hear them smashing off the balconies and breaking against the windscreens of the parked cars below. It was like I was in a daze, just doing whatever I pleased. I heard some people come out of their flats and start shouting, but I just ignored them and carried on. Nobody had seen me and I couldn't give a toss what they thought anyway. And then suddenly I heard David's voice; that snapped me back to reality.

'John, is that you? John! It better not be you, you little bastard!'

I could hear David's heavy footsteps on the stairwell and his voice getting louder and louder. 'John, d'you hear me?! Where are you? John? Is that you?!'

I had nowhere to hide so I put on my best fake voice, trying to make out I was having a conversation with a mate.

'Come on, John, join in with me,' I called, in the deepest voice I could muster. 'Help me chuck the bottles, John. Come on!'

'No! Stop it, stop it,' I replied, in my own, higher-pitched voice, which I tried to make sound as innocent as possible. 'No! I'm not doing that. Stop it, stop it!'

Ridiculously, I kept on throwing the milk bottles over the side as I carried out my little performance, and I only stopped when I heard David about to turn the corner.

'Can you believe what that nutter's gone and done?' I said, looking behind me down the empty balcony, doing my best outraged voice. 'And now he's done a runner!'

'What you talking about, John?' David shouted. 'You're the only nutter around here, and you're a little liar to boot. Get here now!'

David put one of his giant hands on the scruff of my jacket and lifted me off the ground with one big tug before dragging me back to the flat, where Dot was waiting to give me a proper hiding.

'I don't know why he's going off the rails like this,' she sobbed to David, after she'd given me a few smacks on my arse. 'I don't know what to do with him.'

When Gerry got home that evening, Dot told him about my truancy and the milk bottles and he blew his top. He couldn't believe who I was turning into. He didn't want to ask why, he just wanted to make sure it didn't happen again. 'You fat little bastard,' he shouted over and over again in a rage. 'Don't you DARE pull another stunt like that. D'you hear me? DO YOU HEAR ME?'

'Sorry, Dad. I really am sorry. I don't know why I did it.'

'Because you're a little bastard, that's why. Any more of it and you know where the street door is.'

No matter how bad I'd been beforehand, getting picked up by the police or letting those two kids into the flat, he'd never threatened me with the street door. What he said next still echoes in my head.

'You've gone and done it this time. Any more trouble and you can go and live with Jimmy Dolan – do you hear me? Either Jimmy Dolan or the children's home. I don't care which.' That was the first time he'd ever threatened to send me to live with Jimmy Dolan, and it crushed me. Even though I knew he was my biological father, Jimmy was still a virtual stranger to me, and the thought of living with him filled me with such horror I was nearly sick. I'd told myself so many times that nothing had changed in the family that I think I almost believed it; and yet here was Gerry, the man I always considered my real father, saying that he'd be happy to see me gone. The street door was never quite shut after that.

———

I have to say it did the trick, and I started to behave a lot better for a while, settling back into a proper routine, keeping my head down, and staying out of trouble as much as possible. The bullying carried on, but I tried not to let it bother me as much as it had. At the end of primary school, I was off to the Central Foundation Boys' School, which was up by the Old Street roundabout. It was big for an inner-city school, about five hundred boys from the ages of eleven to eighteen, and it had a reputation for being pretty tough. I'd heard all kinds of scare stories about the bigger lads who went there and I nagged Dot not to send me there.

'You'll be fine, John,' she said. 'You're a big, strong lad – you'll have no trouble.'

I didn't believe her, and my nerves were jangling when I set out to walk to school on my first day. I wished I could have taken Butch with me for protection.

I dragged my feet all the way to school and I spent most of my first day wishing I could make myself invisible and hoping I didn't need to go to the toilet, where the older kids were meant to hang out. By the middle of the afternoon I was bursting, and I had to go. I'll never forget the smell when I walked down the long, winding staircase to the toilet block in the basement, and I'm not talking about the stink of the urinals. Clouds of smoke billowed out from under the door, and once inside I could hardly see two paces in front of me, the smoke was that thick. Just as I'd been warned, a gang of older lads ten times scarier than the boys from my estate were hanging around, smoking, swearing and looking for a bit of fun or trouble, most likely both. They all turned to look at me and I gulped. My gold-striped tie was too tight around my neck and I had knots in my stomach.

'Cor, that's a big belly you've got there!' one of the boys called out. 'Been working on that all summer have you? Packing away the pies? What's that fat kid called on *Grange Hill*? Roland? Yeah, that's right, we'll call you Roly from now on.'

I felt my face flush bright red, but thankfully they all just had a good laugh, carried on puffing on their fags and left me alone. Some of them had smuggled in bottles of alcohol, while others were rolling their own long cigarettes; I'd later find out from personal experience that the potent smell wasn't just caused by fag smoke, but weed too. On that first day I got in and out of there as fast as I could, amazed that I hadn't been shown the inside of a toilet bowl. The bigger boys probably didn't fancy their chances of lifting someone of my size upside down.

It took me a while to settle in, which I guess I never properly did. I just never was one for school. I had the same trouble in most of the classes that I'd had before: lack of attention and lots of time spent doodling. And yet again, the only class I could really get my teeth into was Art. The teacher was a laid-back bloke called Mr Glover, who would always let me choose what I wanted to do. He'd leave me alone at my desk, busily sketching my black-and-white pencil drawings, copying pictures of cars or celebrities out of magazines that were piled up at the back of the class. It was the only time I concentrated in school. I'd get so engrossed in whatever I was drawing that the time would fly right by, and I always got a jolt when the bell sounded. Mr Glover was such a good-natured fella that he didn't mind breaking a few rules on my behalf. I was walking past his classroom on my way to Geography one day when I decided I'd rather be doing Art instead, and so I asked him if I could come in.

'Course you can John, as long as you sit quietly. There's a spare seat at the back.' It didn't matter if he was teaching third-, fourth- or even fifth-years, from that day forward he'd always let me join the class and never questioned what other lesson I was missing or had been kicked out of.

He was the only teacher who ever complimented me on my work, and he would keep me behind after class some days and ask what I intended to do when I grew up. Back then I had no clue, and would just brush him off, but just his asking me made me realise that I could do something, that maybe I had a talent I could use. It was the first time any teacher had taken an interest in what I was doing.

Back at home, I still did a fair amount of drawing to keep myself from getting bored, but not as often as I had when I was younger. Gerry had stopped buying comics for me; I was too old I suppose, and he told me that I didn't deserve any special treats, not the way I was carrying on.

It was just doodles, copies and sketches mostly, of whatever caught my eye; and I never really finished what I started. Story of my life, that. It would take me twenty-five years before I learned how to finish one of my drawings. Believe it or not, the drawing that did it was a sketch of my George, and it was the first drawing I ever sold.

Copying comics as a kid. I'd be in a world of my own.

Chapter Seven

I'd like to tell you a bit more about George. He's been making a nuisance of himself, padding around my desk as I write.

'Go and lie down!' I've been telling him. 'Give me a bit of peace and quiet, will you?'

He's sat on the leather chair in Griff's art studio on Rivington Street in Shoreditch, head slumped, looking down his nose at me. 'Fancy yourself as a writer as well now, do you?' the cheeky beggar's expression is saying.

'Matter of fact, I do. Now wind your neck in and go to sleep.'

I'd got as far as telling you that I'd gone to the park with George, on the first morning after I'd taken him on, only to realise I had a big, powerful animal on my hands that needed a lot of looking after. And there I was, barely equipped to look after myself. As we were walking back from the park, George pulling hard against the lead and dragging me along, I was slowly coming to terms with my decision, telling myself it would be alright, that somehow I would manage and then . . . BANG! George tears the lead out of my hand and is off like a shot. I looked up and saw a little tabby cat about thirty yards away, minding its own business, rubbing its back against some railings, unaware at that moment of the barking-mad Staffie coming right for it. I watched in panic as he chased down the cat, who had since realised the situation and bolted off down the street.

'George! Come here!' I shouted, limping after him. 'Come back here, George, you bastard.'

He reappeared a minute or two later, eyes shining and lead trailing between his legs, looking like he'd thoroughly enjoyed his little game.

'You bastard, you absolute bastard!' I told him firmly as I got a hold of his lead and wrapped it round my hand. I was saying it as loudly and fiercely as possible because I wanted to make sure he knew that what he had done must never be repeated.

George lowered his head and crinkled his brow, but looked up at me with what is the best definition of puppy-dog eyes. I could see he was sorry, but he also had a look about him that said: 'Mind you, you can't blame a dog for chasing a cat, can you?'

George and cats just don't mix.

I had to admit he had a point, but I couldn't let him carry on like that. George wasn't under control, and that meant he was a danger to himself, to me and to the public, not to mention all the unfortunate cats in the area. If I'd had my sensible head on, I probably would have taken a cab to the nearest animal rescue centre, held up my hands and said: 'Sorry, can't do it.'

But, like I say, back then, I was about as far away from sensible as you can get. I'd taken George in on instinct. I didn't think about how much it would cost to feed him or anything practical like that, and even though I knew he was going to cause me all kinds of grief, in the few days I'd known him I was already feeling quite fond of George.

I liked having him around in the bedsit, especially after I'd been used to having the place full with Becky and Sam and their sheepdog, and my gut was telling me to keep him. There was something about George that made him unique, something about him that immediately made me feel protective of him. It's hard to describe, but if you meet him, and I hope you do one day, you'll know exactly what I mean.

'We'll work something out,' I told myself, though I didn't know how, not yet.

George followed me around all that evening, and he slept in the crook of my leg again that night. The next day I decided to take him up to my usual spot at Tower Hill tube station, to see if I could manage to earn a few quid for us and get him some food. Sam and Becky had left some cans of dog food behind, but George was always hungry and we were already running low. Anyway, what could go wrong, as long as I kept tight hold of his lead?

'Everything,' I imagined George saying as he watched me clip on his lead, his eyes questioning me. 'Are you asking for trouble?'

'Oi, behave,' I told him. 'Now let's move it.'

George was a pain in the arse all the way there. I was worried about looking after George on my crutches so I'd left them at home, which meant I had to walk slowly and carefully. George didn't like that. He nearly pulled my arm off trying to get me to speed up, and my bad ankle was throbbing with pain as I dug my heels in, and tried to keep myself upright.

'Have a bit of respect for an old man!' I told him.

A few of the homeless guys I knew came up to me as soon as I arrived with George. They already knew a lot about George's previous owner. A couple of them even knew the drunk Scotsman and warned me to be careful.

'I've heard he's going to take a pound off you every time he sees you,' one said. 'You need to watch your back.'

Another told me the Scot was a nasty piece of work and said he had earned a reputation for robbing homeless people. I didn't like the sound of the last one, and I wanted to make sure he wasn't going to get any ideas about me and George.

'I know all about him,' I said, putting it on a bit. 'I'm already on it. I've got a baseball bat with his name on it, written lengthways, sideways, back to front and upside down. If he tries to threaten me or take George back, I'll show it to him, good and proper.'

I'm not a violent man by nature and I had no intention of attacking anyone with a baseball bat, but I wanted that word to be put around that I wasn't easy meat, and I knew I could rely on the guys on the street to do that for me. That is one of the many heartwarming things I've learned over the years about the homeless community: the vast majority mind each other's backs. When you've been on the bones of your backside and sleeping rough, you learn the importance of solidarity and looking after people in the same boat as you. I'd put the word out there now, and I knew I could rely on the other guys on the street to make it travel, to help protect both me and George.

My usual routine at this point in time was to walk around the entrance to the underground, going up to passers-by and politely asking if they could spare any change. Having been brought up by proud parents like Gerry and Dot, I was very embarrassed about being in that position. The only way I made it right in my head was to think of myself as an entertainer asking for a tip, so I always tried to engage the people I approached in a bit of banter or make them smile.

'How are you today?' I'd say. 'Going anywhere nice? Cost you a pound for a piggyback.' Silly stuff really, but I would never have dreamed of just holding out my hand miserably, or standing there looking threatening in any way. Even when I was at my most desperate, I always tried to put a smile on my face and did my best to make conversation.

Most people would look straight through me and pretend I wasn't there. Others would look embarrassed and fish out a bit of change for me before scuttling past as quickly as they could. Only the minority actually engaged in conversation and treated me like a fellow human being. I don't blame them for thinking that there must be something wrong with a beggar or a homeless person. It can be scary wondering why they've ended up on the street, that they must have done something terrible or have some dark side to their character. I understand that, but it's not even close to the truth in the vast majority of cases. Having been one myself and been friends with many, I know that beggars and home-less people are just the same as everybody else. They are the sort of people who are horrified at the thought of a dog being abused or a mad Scot robbing and threatening vulnerable people. Most of them are on the streets because they are unlucky people and have been dealt a bad hand in life, often through no fault of their own. That doesn't mean they don't have feelings like everybody else, or that they are inferior human beings who don't deserve basic respect.

Despite putting on my cheeriest smile and doing my best to make the process of begging as painless as possible for all concerned, I hated it at the best of times. I only begged because I was hungry and needed a cup of tea, but I found putting myself at the mercy of others very humiliating and very bad for the soul.

Optimistically, I thought having George with me when I went out begging might make it easier. I know a lot of people are understandably wary of breeds like Staffies as there's such a lot of bad press about them, but because he was so handsome I was hoping he would be an asset.

'You gonna turn on the charm?' I said to him now, as I pitched up at Tower Hill tube station. 'I need you to dazzle 'em, George.'

He cocked his leg up against a wall and shot me a look that said: 'Piss off! How am I gonna do that?'

Within the first five minutes of us sitting down, George was roving around, sniffing people, barking, dragging me all over the pavement and generally making a terrible nuisance of himself. I kept on trying to make him sit and calm down, but he was having none of it. Anything and everything triggered him – the growl of a taxi's diesel engine, a flutter of pigeons, even a strong breeze. He just wouldn't sit still. The worst thing of all was that some of the commuters who walked past us looked genuinely nervous of George, which I felt horrible about. I obviously wasn't in control of him the way an animal like him needed to be controlled, and that wasn't right. We didn't stay long.

'You need to learn some manners,' I told George as we walked around together. 'For one thing, ladies don't like it when you sniff their skirts or jump up at them. I'm gonna have to teach you to behave.'

He looked at me long and hard, like he was wondering how a fella like me was going to manage that.

'Up to the job, are you?' his expression said. 'Gentleman John, are we?'

'I'll teach you,' I said. 'Watch and learn, George. There's more to me than meets the eye. I'll show you.'

We started heading back to the flat, and for a few minutes I was relieved to find that George was walking quite well on the lead. We were doing alright up until we turned the corner of Royal Mint Street, and then a black cat scorched out from an alleyway a few yards ahead of us. The cat ran across the road and George went for it like the *Looney Tunes* Coyote chasing the Roadrunner. He took off so fast, and he was so strong, that he jolted the lead clean out of my hand and chicaned me into a lamppost.

'Stop, George! You bastard! Come here! Stop, you bastard!' I shouted, trying to sound as stern as possible. 'Stop, you stupid bastard!'

He didn't even look back at me, and I watched in fright as he streaked out into the road in front of a black cab, forcing it to swerve. The cabbie slammed his horn, waved his fist at me, and shouted: 'Why don't you fucking keep control of him?' while the cat escaped over a wall, leaving George barking on the opposite side of the road.

'Sorry, mate!' I waved to the cabbie, who scowled, shook his head and drove off.

'STAY THERE, YOU BAAASTARD GEORGE,' I shouted across the road. 'WAIT! DON'T YOU MOVE! YOU HEAR ME? STAY THERE!'

He was looking right at me while I waited for the road to clear so I could cross over and retrieve him. It was obvious that I wanted him to stay and wait, but George either didn't get it or had other ideas. He ran straight back over the road, frightening the living daylights out of a bloke on a bike who called me a fucking twat, which I couldn't argue with. I was unbelievably relieved to have him back on the lead – as well as a little spooked – and by the time I'd shoved George back inside the flat I had beads of sweat on my forehead and my hands were shaking.

'You'll be out the street door if you do that again,' I warned him. 'Haven't you been taught anything at all?'

He sniffed the air and started licking himself.

'I'll take that as a no,' I said. 'And you can stop that right now.'

I'd angrily picked up one of my crutches as I spoke and was shaking it at him; George flinched and whimpered and stopped what he was doing almost immediately. It didn't take a genius to see that he might have been given a good kicking or two by somebody he'd encountered in his past. It was horrible to see him shrink like that, and it burned a hole in my chest. I guiltily dropped the crutch and went over to start ruffling his head. Wherever he'd come from, I reckoned George deserved a break. I knew what it was like to be down on your luck, and I really wanted to help him. I'd trained Butch as a kid, and even though that was a long time ago, I knew I could train George if I put my mind to it. Also, I knew that if I didn't train him, I might have to let him go, and that was an outcome I could handle less and less.

He was sitting beside me, staring at me in a way that was a bit unnerving, like he was trying to read my thoughts. That's the thing I'd really noticed about George. He was obviously incredibly intelligent, and he had this charisma and presence that I'd never experienced before in a dog. It wouldn't be true to say he was almost human; that would be going too far. At times, though, I thought he had more brains than I had. It was impossible not to respond when he looked at me in that quizzical way. I honestly wouldn't have been surprised if he'd suddenly opened his mouth and barked at me: 'You alright, mate?'

'Yes, George,' I found myself saying, answering his unasked question. 'I'm alright, mate. Just thinking, that's all. Just working out what to do next.'

He looked down; as if he understood he needed to let me have some time to sort my thoughts out.

Nobody seemed to know how the mad Scot had come to have George, but I imagined it couldn't have been a pretty story, not with a character like him involved. Thinking about my own upbringing was reinforcing what a huge responsibility I had taken on with George. I didn't just have to look after him on a daily basis, I had to teach him how to behave and survive in the big wide world. I'd inherited him, like Dot and Gerry had inherited me. I had to do my best, just like they did when I needed a home and a family.

I would have to train him to behave off the lead, so I could walk on my crutches without fear of being pulled over or losing control of him.

'I've got a plan, George. How about we train you up so you don't need that old lead of yours?'

At the mention of the word 'lead' George began sniffing around the bedsit looking for it, thinking I was taking him for a walk.

'No, forget about that, George,' I told him. 'Come with me, I've got a good idea.'

My flat was close to the Highway, which is a very big main road leading out from Tower Bridge towards Essex. I decided that was going to be George's training ground. It was always really busy, but I knew it like the back of my hand and if I could teach him to cross that road safely without a lead, I knew I could teach him anything.

When we set off, my arthritis had kicked in really badly and I was leaning heavily on my crutches. I knew this wasn't going to be easy, and I was feeling nervous from the moment we left the bedsit, but it had to be done. The simple fact was that if George wasn't trained and couldn't walk off the lead, I couldn't keep him.

'Right, this is the deal,' I said to him as we reached the pavement. 'You stay with me now and you can stay with me for good. Any nonsense and you'll be out the street door.'

I surprised myself by saying that out loud. The words tasted bad in my mouth. Already, we'd been through a fair amount together and I was feeling more and more attached to him. I think he felt the same way about me, because he was watching my every move and listening to me carefully, like he really wanted to understand and do the right thing.

'Good boy, George,' I told him. 'Stay close, boy. That's a good boy. Stay close to me. Nice one.'

It was all going well so far. George was walking beside me and was turning and looking at me so often I was now starting to worry about him walking into something rather than running off. Even so, every time we turned a corner my eyes were everywhere, scanning the streets and pavements, praying there were no cats about. If George started to stray more than a foot or two away from me, I shouted at him in my deepest, sternest voice: 'George! Come here! Oi! Get here, NOW!'

I kept repeating myself over and over again and George responded well, even if he did seem to have the words 'You've told me that already. I'm a dog, not a goldfish' written on his face. I knew from having Butch that it's not what you say to a dog that matters, it's how you say it. Projecting your voice and sounding authoritative is what works, as does using the right body language and looking like you're in charge. Come to think of it, I'd probably learnt that from Gerry too. He very rarely had to lay a finger on me; his pantomime baddie voice had always been its own punishment.

George wagged his tail when I spoke in a softer, quieter voice. 'Good boy, George! You're doing well.'

It was rush hour when we reached the Highway, which probably sounds like lunacy, but it meant that although the road would be really busy, the traffic wouldn't be moving too quickly. This was a good combination for George. There needed to be an element of danger for him to learn the rules of the road, but hopefully not too much.

'STAY!' I boomed as we approached a pedestrian crossing in front of a furniture shop. 'Do you hear me, George? STAY.'

The traffic was loud and I could see George was on his guard, ears pointing up and his eyes everywhere. That's what I wanted. I needed him to smell the danger, and then hopefully his instincts would make him stay close to me.

I thought it was a good idea at the time, but when I look back I can imagine what George would say. 'Are you having a laugh? You really think that's gonna work?'

I suppose that's one of my personality traits. Even at the lowest points in my life, I always had flashes of optimism – or maybe they were moments of madness?

Anyhow, I was definitely in a glass-half-full sort of mood that day, and I was sure this was going to work.

'Come on, George. Stay with me, boy. Stay. STAY! GEORGE! GEORGE! COME BACK HERE, YOU BASTARD! GEORGE! YOU BAAAASTAAAARD!'

George was off, darting across the Highway like a marble in a pinball machine. He wasn't looking at the traffic at all; his focus was on a bloody big ginger cat that was prancing along a shop windowsill on the opposite side of the road. I watched, mortified and scared witless as drivers had to slow down, swerve or slam on their brakes to avoid hitting George. A white van nearly hit the car in front, and I got a few choice hand signals to thank me.

I was still rooted to the spot in fear, my heart pounding, but before I could even catch my breath George decided to come back for more. He must have lost the cat, and I watched in panic as he just turned on his heel and ran back towards me, weaving through the traffic all over again. In a flash, he was back by my side, panting furiously and looking as shocked as I was at what he'd just done.

'You're a BAD DOG, George. Stay there. Do you hear me? STAY!'

It was an absolute miracle he didn't cause a serious accident or get run over. I got one of my crutches and smacked the pavement as hard as I could, making as much noise as I could and going absolutely mental so he knew how bad his behaviour was.

'YOU BASTARD! BAD GEORGE!' I bellowed over and over again. He pinned back his ears, furrowed his brow and gave a loud yelp. It was pitiful really, and I definitely didn't enjoy treating him like that, but I was relieved by his reaction.

For all I knew he could have turned on me. Homeless dogs who have been mistreated have that streak in them – they don't always take criticism well, let's say. But he took it on the chin, and that's when I knew we were going to be alright. I got a few dirty looks from passers-by who saw me shout so loudly at George, and I know there will be some people out there who don't agree with what I did. I didn't react in anger and I wasn't venting on him. Learning not to chase cats and run across roads would potentially save his life down the line. From that day on George has never chased a cat again and these days, even if a cat comes within arm's reach he won't move until I command him to. He doesn't go darting over roads anymore like a total maniac either. I only have to raise my voice to remind him.

'Ain't that, right George?' I've just said to him. He's woken up on Griff's leather chair now and is looking very comfortable and smug. 'You can wipe that look off your face. I'm saying what a silly bastard you were.'

Of course, at the time, I had no idea that in trying to

save George's life I would ultimately save my own. George was a lucky fella, and his luck was about to start rubbing off on me, but I still had to wait a while for it to happen.

George gave me the fright of my life that day he ran out into the road.

Chapter Eight

'I've got you a doctor's appointment, John,' Dot announced one day.

'What for, Mum?'

'It's to get your weight checked, son, that's all,' she replied matter-of-factly. She made it sound as if it was a routine check-up, but of course it wasn't.

By the time I was coming up to my second year of secondary school, I was bigger than I had ever been.

My mum never discussed my weight with me, but she'd obviously decided it was time to act. I was still boxing on and off, but I wasn't getting any slimmer. If anything I was getting bigger. When we went for the appointment, I was so embarrassed just to stand in front of the local GP with my shirt off while he took my measurements. He made me stand on the scales, moving the weights further up until they balanced out at thirteen stone and four pounds. I was four foot four inches tall! I was clinically obese, and the doctor told Dot he was worried about the serious effect and strain my weight was having on my heart. He decided that I needed specialist help. I didn't ask any questions; I just wanted to put my shirt back on and get out of there as quickly as I could.

Pretty soon after, Mum told me I would be going into Barts Hospital for a few weeks over the summer holidays; 'to help me lose a bit of weight' was how she phrased it. I didn't like the sound of going into hospital for any period of time, but then I didn't like being fat either so I just nodded in agreement.

Barts Hospital is located in Smithfield in the City of London. It's a big old building, and there's a Norman church attached to it that Mum said was nearly a thousand years old. She said it survived the Great Fire of London and the Blitz so it was the safest place in the world. As we approached the entrance, I saw people were throwing money into a fishpond. I put my suitcase down for a minute to look in the water.

'Cor, look at the size of them goldfish, Mum!' I said.

'They're koi carp, dear,' an old lady corrected me as she tottered past on her Zimmer frame.

I was fascinated and scared stiff all at the same time – the building was unlike any other I'd seen. I've now drawn many buildings in London but I've never tried to replicate the detail and grandeur of Barts. The surroundings were lovely too – it was like a scene out of a history book – but I didn't have time to appreciate it all as I was more concerned about what I was walking into.

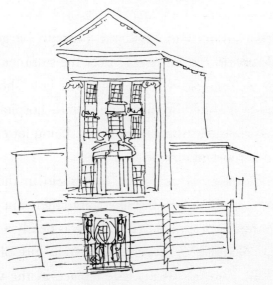

The Henry VIII gatehouse at Barts. The oldest surviving part of the hospital.

The sterile smell and the heat on the ward gave me a headache, and the nurses in their starched uniforms, pushing their noisy metal trolleys, made me feel on edge all the time. I was put in a bed next to a lad of about fifteen who had a broken leg, and the four other kids on the ward were all having their tonsils out. We didn't have much in common, apart from the fact we were all as homesick as hell and were trying not to show it. It was my first time away from home.

————————

The nurses would get me up at 7 a.m. and have me running around the grounds and up and down the stairs, which were covered in the most magnificent murals by William Hogarth as I later found out. After my morning workout I'd see a physiotherapist, and then there would be a session with a specialist doctor. On the first day he put me on a kind of exercise bike that was attached to a speedometer. I did seven miles the first time I went on it, even though I was puffing and wheezing like a chain-smoking miner.

My mum and dad were allowed to visit in the afternoons. Quite often, though, only Dot came along. I don't think her and Gerry were getting on very well at the time, and I didn't dare ask why. I didn't mind when it was just her; I was just really pleased to see a friendly face. She usually stayed for a few hours in between her cleaning shifts. I got the impression that she would have stayed longer if she could, to prolong her time away from President House and from Gerry. Dot would gossip for hours with another mother whose kid was on my ward, while I sat in bed doodling or copying pictures from one of the old magazines left around. It didn't matter if it was *Shoot!* or *Smash Hits*, I might have a go at drawing a football or Simon Le Bon's head; I wasn't fussy.

I stayed in hospital for two weeks, and then I went as a day patient for about three months. Crisps, chocolate and fizzy drinks were all banned from my diet and I was only allowed one portion of chips a week! Dot used to cook dinners like sausage and mash or liver and bacon and everything that could be fried was, so that had to stop too. Now it was all fruit and veg, boil-in-the-bag fish with parsley sauce and poached eggs, which I soon got used to and started to enjoy.

The weight fell off me, and by the Christmas of my second year of secondary school I was just over nine stone. I was no longer 'the fat kid', which came as a huge relief. Losing just over four stone was life-changing, and I can remember staring at myself in the mirror and not quite believing my eyes. I pulled my shoulders back and immediately felt taller. I felt like a different person: I still had my art and Butch, but for the first time, I was in good shape. Everything was lining up beautifully.

In hindsight I can see that although losing weight was a really positive thing in itself, curiously my behaviour at school got steadily worse. I became an even cockier, cheekier little version of my old self. Maybe it was my teenage hormones kicking in but whatever it was, I couldn't shake it. I grew tired of school, and even Mr Glover, who still let me sit in the back of his Art classes, couldn't keep me there. 'Fancy a day off?' a big lad asked me one morning. 'Want to tag along with us?'

I knew the big lad was part of a gang of older boys that congregated in the tower-block staircases or the underground car park, and they were rarely in school. I also knew that they were into harder things than smoking cigarettes. The big lad would sniff Tippex thinner and tins of lighter fuel, and on the rare occasions he was in school he'd have a can up the arm of his blazer and would sniff away in the classroom, or he'd tip the thinner on his sleeve and place his lips over the wet patch and inhale.

None of this put me off kicking about with him and his little gang. Secretly, I was quite pleased with myself to be invited into the gang. It was the sort of thing that didn't happen to me when I was fat, and I didn't need asking twice.

'Let John have a go on that,' the big lad said as soon as we met his mates in a dark corner of the car park.

One of the lads had a bottle of Tippex thinner which he handed to me, and they all started telling me to pour it onto my sleeve and inhale.

'It's a laugh, John,' the big lad said. 'Have a go!'

I did it without thinking. I couldn't see what harm a little hit on a bottle of stuff like that could do. You could buy it in the corner shop or nick it from the stationery cupboard at school, so it was hardly illegal. Straight away I felt my head swirl and I found it quite amusing. I knew from past experience that bunking off wasn't always this much fun, and I was more than happy to join in with the lads as they all egged each other on to sniff more and more. We wandered around the streets, jumping on and off buses, talking a load of crap to each other and generally wasting the day. The hours passed really quickly, and the next day I was back for more of the same, or so I thought.

'Here, have a go on that,' the big lad said again, but this time he gave me a can of lighter fuel.

His mates were all giggling. It was only 9 a.m. but they'd already had a sniff on the gas and were obviously really enjoying themselves. They showed me how to do it and I could tell this was a lot more powerful than the Tippex thinner. My mind felt like it bent a bit. The sensation was instant, and this time the day passed even quicker. It was like flicking a switch and taking your head somewhere else, where the sharp edges are knocked off your vision and feelings, and everything goes a little bit blurred or hazy, or somehow not quite normal. I liked the feeling of being not quite normal.

I started sniffing Tippex and aerosols on and off for weeks, if not months. I'd bunk off with the lads nearly all the time, making an appearance at school only when Dot had had a phone-call or I'd been threatened by Gerry that if I didn't pull my socks up I'd be booted out the street door and into a children's home, or sent off to live with Jimmy Dolan.

I know I made Gerry and Dot's life a misery at times, but I loved them to bits and I couldn't imagine not living with them. I hated myself when I made Dot cry and I couldn't stand it when Gerry lost his temper and shouted at me. The teachers could scream and shout until they were blue in the face and I'd just shrug it off, but when Gerry gave me an ear-bashing it really shook me up, because I cared about him and what he thought of me. More importantly, I wasn't scared enough by Gerry's threats to stop misbehaving.

The older I got, the easier it became for me to slip under the radar when I wanted to. By the time I was fifteen, they were in their mid-forties – not exactly old by today's standards, but they'd brought up four kids on next to no money, and Gerry in particular was starting to run out of energy with me. Let's face it, who could blame him?

Eventually I started to suffer from headaches but, as stupid as it sounds now, I didn't link them to my solvent abuse. Dot became very concerned because the symptoms I was suffering from were severe, and similar to the effects of migraines, which she suffered from herself. She took me off to a GP who asked about my headaches and when they started. I lied and we left with a prescription for serious painkillers. I took the maximum dose every day, and carried on sniffing glue regularly. Bizarrely I still wondered why my head was hurting!

One day Dot came home from work, pulled the plug out of the television and gave me an almighty wallop around the earhole.

'What was that for?!'

'I'll show you,' she said, shaking with temper.

She opened her handbag and pulled out a glue bag.

'I found it in your bedroom.'

'Oh. I'm so sorry, Mum . . .'

'I'll give you sorry. Headaches, you said! Didn't know what was causing them! I'll give you a bloody headache, John . . .'

I thought she was going to give me another smack round the head, but instead she slumped onto the sofa and started crying. I told her I was sorry over and over again. She looked tired out and worried sick. I hated to see her like that, and I tried to limit the damage.

'It's only for a laugh,' I said. 'I didn't think you'd find out. I'm not addicted. Nothing like that. I don't even think the headaches are related to the glue . . .'

Dot cried all night long, and she took me back to the GP the next day and put the glue bag on his desk.

'I think I've found the cause of them headaches,' she said. 'And I want John to get some help. He won't listen to me or his father.'

A few weeks later I was given an appointment with a 'head doctor'. Nobody used the word psychologist or psychiatrist or anything like that back then. It was just a 'head doctor' who was going to talk to me about why I'd want to do something as stupid as sniffing glue. When I walked into the clinic I was expecting to see just one doctor, but there was a semicircle of half a dozen men and women, some in white coats and all looking very serious. I had to sit on a chair facing them, while they all took it in turns to ask me questions.

'Are you unhappy at home?' one of them asked.

'No,' I replied. 'My mum and dad spoil me rotten.'

This time I wasn't lying. I loved my mum and dad and I couldn't imagine living anywhere else. They clothed, fed me, and if ever I wanted something they got it for me. Other kids I grew up with were left to fend for themselves. Their houses were dirty, their mums were always drunk or their dads would beat them up. My life wasn't like that, and I really believed it when I told the doctors that my childhood was idyllic.

'Have you got problems at school?' another asked.

'No,' I said after a pause. 'I just hate it.'

'What do you hate?'

'Everything.'

'There must be something you like. Try to name one thing you like.'

'Art class, I guess. That's it. I hate everything else.'

———————

I made a promise to Dot that I would stop hanging out with the gang and stop with the solvents. I made it through to Christmas and as a treat I was given a set of paint-based pens which came up like watercolours when you dipped them in water and used them on cardboard. The results were fantastic, and I started doing some original drawings instead of just copying from comics. At times I felt like one of those old painters with his easel and paintbrush; the only difference was I was using felt-tip pens. Copying just didn't do the colours justice. They were usually pictures of barbarians or Gothic-style people, like the Addams Family. I'd draw stuff like a really ugly daughter with long, witchy hair, a creepy grandmother and a set of weird parents with black rims around their eyes. Nothing was ever finished and they were all just sketches, but I wasn't drawing them for anyone else; they were just for my own pleasure and to see how far I'd come.

One day Dot slipped one of my drawings in her handbag because she wanted to show it off to her friends at work. She was cleaning offices near Smithfield meat market, and one of the blokes from the market happened to see my picture as Dot passed it around.

'Who drew that?' he asked her, looking really interested.

'My son John,' she said proudly.

'Well, can you ask him if he fancies designing us a logo?'

This man had been looking for an artist to design a trademark for his company, which he wanted to put on the side of his fleet of vans.

'Will you pay him?' Dot asked.

'A fiver for every van it goes on,' he said.

'I'll ask him,' Dot said shrewdly, knowing that this could earn me quite a few quid if I pulled it off.

When she told me all this I was really excited. This was the first time that anyone who wasn't in my immediate family – or Mr Glover – had expressed an interest in my art.

I got to work straight away, playing with styles and images. I wanted something really original, something that would make it stand out.

I decided to bunk off school and go to Smithfield meat market to see what other companies' logos looked like. This time I didn't feel guilty about missing school – I figured if I was going to be a famous artist then this was a step in the right direction.

When I got home I sat down and tried to draw the logo, but it just wasn't coming. Maybe it was the pressure of having to produce something on demand, or the fact that at the time, I still didn't have enough faith in my ability. In the end I drew a picture of a jolly butcher in a striped apron, with his arm over a happy chicken. It was corny and I knew I could probably do better, but I was hopeful it would be good enough for the logo. After all, the market trader had asked for me especially. But when I showed it to Dot she took a quick look and said: 'I don't think so, but nice try.' And that was the end of that. My first potential commission and I couldn't deliver the goods. What hurt most of all, though, was Dot's reaction. She'd always been a champion of my art, but it was as if she was embarrassed by what I'd produced – she never even took the drawing with her to work.

Chapter Nine

'Shut up, you prick!' I shouted as I pressed the talk button on my CB radio. All my mates were cracking up laughing as we yet again destroyed the conversation between the two lovers.

It was the era when CBs were all the rage, and for fifteen-year-old boys like us it was the Twitter of its day. Having conversations over the airwaves with each other was a real novelty, but the best thing was when a few kids would come round my house, when Gerry and Dot were out, and gather around my radio to listen into other peoples' conversations. People would arrange fights over the CBs, and be very specific about the time and place to meet, what they'd be wearing, and even what they looked like. Me and my mates would all be chipping in and goading them on, saying stuff like: 'Don't turn up, you mug, he'll batter you! You sound like you couldn't punch your way out of a wet paper bag! You couldn't open a door without pulling a muscle!'

By far the funniest thing was when we'd listen to a couple of lovers whispering sweet nothings to each other. The beauty of it was the man wouldn't be able to hear the insults we were giving him while he was talking to his girlfriend; if the signal from your aerial was more powerful than the other person's who was on the same channel, you could talk over the top of them. When the girlfriend started asking what was going on and why somebody was calling her fella a prick, we'd all listen and snigger as their conversation fell apart.

'Derek,' she'd say. 'As you're talking, someone else is talking over the top of you.'

'What you saying, babes?'

'They're calling you a prick.'

'Who else is on this channel?' Derek would shout. 'That you, Trevor?'

At that point we'd all slam in with insults. 'Here, Derek, your bird's ugly. What a minger! Is she Cyclops's sister?'

Sometimes we'd be really spiteful and would follow them all over the forty channels as they tried to get away from us. In the end they had no choice but to hang up. It beat the hell out of sitting around at home alone with Butch.

The more we messed around like this, the more obsessed we got. It got to the point where we would climb up on roofs all around the area and nick aerials belonging to other CB radio users if they looked better than ours. Then we'd use them to boost the signal on our radios. Getting access to the rooftops was easy – we bought FB2 keys for the gates guarding them from the local locksmiths, who were happy for the business. They didn't ask and we didn't tell, it was as simple as that.

Stealing the aerials was just one of a number of things we did back then to stave off the boredom. My mates and I were now regularly smoking weed and we spent many a happy afternoon getting nicely stoned around each other's houses, listening to music on those bulky cassette players – stuff like Fine Young Cannibals and Public Image Ltd. Whose house we all went to depended on whose mum and dad were away at work and with Gerry still working mornings as a dustman, it was rarely ever mine. I hated being cooped up at home with him though and would take Butch out as much as I could. He was around six at this point and had barely grown any bigger since being a puppy. He was still a little nervous too, and if I let him off the lead he would barely leave my side. Every time my mates saw me walking him around the estate they would take the mick mercilessly.

'Oh, nice gay dog, John. Real butch.' Crap like that. It couldn't have bothered me less.

One evening, I was around the flat of a friend of mine who lived in President House. When we'd finished off with our usual nonsense on the CB, he told me about a pair of bolt cutters his dad kept under his bed. His mum and dad were out that evening and so we nipped into the bedroom to grab them and worked out what to do next. There was a local park nearby whose gates were padlocked at night and we thought it would be a laugh to cut it off. No more than that. We had no intention of nicking anything – we just thought it would be funny. We ran down to the park gates and after only a few seconds working on the padlock my mate suddenly yelled out: 'John! Old Bill!'

I spun round and there was a police car on the street nearby with two policemen inside, both looking in our direction. We hadn't bothered to check, bunch of idiots. As quick as you like, I dropped the bolt cutters and we both ran off, darting in opposite directions.

I don't know where my mate went, but I ended up on a local estate around the corner called Midway that was maze-like in its design. Luckily, I knew it like the back of my hand and I had these two coppers falling all over themselves trying to catch me. I'd grown out of my childhood asthma by then and could really run.

Eventually I jumped a whole flight of stairs, rather than run down them one by one, crossed Goswell Road and ran towards the safety of President House. The next minute I was frantically banging on our street door.

'What you making all that fucking noise with the letter box for?' Gerry shouted.

'I need a crap, Dad. Please let me in. Please.' It was the best excuse I could come up with. I popped into the bathroom, so Gerry didn't think I was lying, trying to keep my heavy-breathing under wraps, and then went straight to bed. Once I'd caught my breath, I lay under my duvet, giggling to myself at the thought of getting away from the police. As far as I was concerned it was a middle finger to the Old Bill.

By midnight Dot and Gerry had gone to bed too and the house was very quiet, but the silence was suddenly shattered by the sound of an almighty knock on our door. It wasn't a letter box knock this time – it was a fist banging hard on the door. Nobody knocked on our door that late. And nobody knocked with a fist.

Straight away I knew it must be the police. My mate had obviously been nicked and he must have grassed me up and given them my address.

I could hear Gerry cursing under his breath as he made his way to the door, cursing even more as he opened the bolts across the door, and cursing louder still when he saw two of the Met's finest standing before him.

'Have you got a John Dolan living here?' one of them said.

'What's he fucking done now?' I heard Gerry reply.

'We're not sure yet. It's in connection to damage to property. It might even be breaking and entering.'

'What, burglary?'

'Possibly. That's why we need to talk to him. Is he in?'

'Yes, just wait there.'

Before Gerry could even make his way to the bedroom I was on my feet, throwing my clothes on, and I met him halfway down the passage. Sheepishly, I looked him in the eye and said: 'Sorry Dad.'

'I'll give you fucking sorry when you get home, you bastard,' was Gerry's reply.

The next thing I knew the policemen slapped a pair of handcuffs on me and led me down the stairwell to their police van. It was about a ten-minute drive to Kings Cross police station, and all I could think of was getting hold of my mate and smacking him hard in the mouth, and the trouble I'd be in when I got back home.

I was charged with criminal damage, which isn't the Great Train Robbery by any stretch, but that still didn't stop the judge at Clerkenwell court handing me a £30 fine, which Gerry had to pay.

'You little bastard,' he said when he handed the notes to me out of his hard-earned wages.

Over the next couple of weeks, if not months, Gerry wouldn't let up. Every time he laid eyes on me he'd be muttering 'bastard' under his breath. As much as I could, I tried to stay out of the flat, taking Butch on huge long walks or sometimes spending a couple of days round a mate's house. When Gerry got really angry, as he did often after a drink, he'd threaten me with the street door again, or say that he was happy to send me off to live with Jimmy Dolan. That still scared the life out of me. Even though I'd got to know Jimmy a little better now, I still didn't know him well and I didn't want to live with him.

I'd met him some more over the last few years and he'd told me about his second-hand office furniture business that he ran with his dad, a bit of a character who everybody called Mad Jimmy. Doesn't take a genius to guess how he got that name. He told me it was doing really well, and asked if I wanted to help out occasionally, which seemed like a good way to make a bit of extra pocket money. It was no big deal. There was no dramatic father-and-son stuff going on; he was just Jimmy Dolan to me, same as he always had been, and we got on fine when I worked for him shifting furniture on the weekends.

In my last year of school, I was placed in a special unit for problem kids from all over London. My attention in class had never picked up, and even though Mr Glover was still doing everything he could to help me, I was becoming more and more of a nuisance. It was better off for all concerned that I left. The new place was more like being at college than school, and we were treated like young adults instead of kids. You could play the guitar or take cookery lessons if you wanted, and there was a smoking room where we'd all sit smoking our Benson & Hedges after class. I went in every day, but really I was just biding my time, counting the days until I was allowed to leave officially.

When the exams took place in May of my last year, I can remember walking into a big hall with loads of other kids, and a teacher announcing: 'If there is anybody here today who does not wish to sit the examination, please leave now and let the others who do want to work proceed.'

I was the first to stand up, and it created a domino effect as one by one several of the other kids stood up too, until about a dozen of us walked out the door. When my final day of school came a few weeks later, I walked out of the gates without a single qualification. I could draw pretty well but that was about it. It didn't bother me though – I was convinced that this was where my life really began. Now I could do anything I wanted, and I was looking forward to seeing what happened next.

A lot of the kids I grew up with settled down young and started having kids very early, which I couldn't see myself doing. I'd never even had a girlfriend, and unfortunately by the time I left school I was as fat as I had been before I went into Barts, so I was unlikely to get one any time soon. I think the weight had only stayed off me for a year at most before I got into weed and started eating all the time, drifting way off the diet. Looking the way I did, I didn't have the self-confidence to ask girls out.

Plenty of school leavers went to work in the rag trade around Clerkenwell, and a few of my mates got jobs in a big shoe factory down the road on Margery Street, gluing the soles on shoes. I couldn't see myself doing that – I hated the idea of doing the same thing over and over again every day of the week – but I didn't have any other plans. I just imagined that somehow, something would turn up and everything would work out fine for me. Naive really.

All I wanted to do was hang around with my mates, listening to music, smoking puff and lazing about. Dot and Gerry had other ideas. They hated seeing me lazing around the house and started putting me under pressure to get a job. Without a single qualification to my name it wasn't easy, and so when Jimmy Dolan offered to give me more work with his office furniture firm they reluctantly agreed that I should take it, even though Dot made it clear she wanted me to get a 'proper job' as soon as possible.

The more time I'd spent with Jimmy, the more I'd come to understand that he was a decent bloke who seemed to genuinely care about me. I came to consider him as a kind of old family friend. When he made the offer, I was more than happy to accept, because if nothing else it would get Dot and Gerry off my case.

This time round Jimmy had me 'carding', which meant going around the city handing out cards that said 'Good Prices Paid for New and Used Office Furniture'. I really started enjoying the work, especially earning my own money, but the problem was that it wasn't regular. I might work two weeks on and then have a week off, and when I was off I was smoking more dope than ever, because I could now afford to buy bigger quantities. I'd spend whole days just sat at home, smoking and sleeping. Every now and then I'd do some press-ups and weights – mostly out of guilt – and that did help shift some of the weight I was carrying, but it wasn't enough. Sleep was always more tempting than working out. What I didn't realise was that I was about to get one hell of a wake-up call.

Chapter Ten

At the age of eighteen, I was remanded to Feltham Young Offenders Institution. I was running a scam with a friend, where I would forge the signatures in stolen savings books and take out £50 or £100 at a time from the bank or post office. The law finally caught up with me and I was sent down for six months on deception charges.

It was December 1989, the Berlin Wall had just come down and Nelson Mandela was about to be released from Robben Island. I figured I was lucky. I lived in a free country and I'd been given a fair hearing. Dot and Gerry could barely look at me throughout the trial. They were more or less done with me by then.

I'd heard Feltham was a very tough place, but I told myself that at least it wasn't an adult prison, and I wouldn't be in there for long. I was just a petty, stupid crook, not a violent thug or anything like that. I'd received a short

125

sentence and would soon be able to put the whole sorry episode behind me and get on with living the rest of my life.

As it was, they turned out to be the toughest six months of my life, and I'm saying that now, as a forty-two-year old who's seen the inside of nearly every prison in Greater London, and a few more besides.

The ordeal started before I even arrived at Feltham, when I was taken from the court to a huge holding cell in Lambeth, South London. There were about fifty young offenders from all over London packed inside, and as soon as I looked at them I realised I wasn't half as streetwise as I thought I was. Some of them looked like proper gangsters, all mean eyes, bulging muscles, scars and gnashing teeth. They could have throttled me with one bare hand. An Asian guy – quite a big chap – walked in wearing a flashy suit and a nice watch. The next minute eight Jamaican guys jumped up, started attacking him and ripped the watch right off his wrist. The police who were outside the cell must have turned a blind eye. This was a taste of what lay ahead for me at Feltham – I knew it wasn't going to be pretty.

From the Lambeth holding cells we were all put into a 'sweat box', which is basically a van with lots of small compartments in it, and then we were herded like cattle across the city to Feltham, out near Heathrow. If you thought you knew what this was like from watching *Scum* with Ray Winstone like I did, think again. The reality is ten times worse; my palms and my forehead were drenched with sweat and I spent the whole journey wracked by fear. It lasted forty minutes and I was absolutely shitting myself the whole way there.

When we finally reached the prison we were all led to a side room, where you had to wait for your name to be called out. All the guys were sizing each other up and you could feel the aggression and testosterone pulsing through the air. I was way, way out of my depth here.

'John Dolan,' a screw called. I had to step out of the side room and go up to a counter that an officer sat behind. I gave him my address and details, and then I was taken to another holding room where I had to give up all my personal effects and change from my civvies into a coarse blue T-shirt, tracksuit bottoms, and old, recycled underpants and socks that must have been used by about fifty other men before me. The socks were thick and woollen, and if your feet weren't sweaty or stinky or riddled with athlete's foot and fungal infections, they would be before long. I was then given a bed sheet pack, a plastic cup and some cutlery before being taken to my cell. I was biting my lip and on the verge of tears as I was led there, but I knew that showing emotion would be seen as a sign of weakness, and I couldn't afford to be seen as an easy target in this place. By the time I reached my single cell on the ground floor I was a number, a barcode being processed.

I soon found out I was surrounded by fellas who were doing time for murders and armed robbery; really violent men who I was terrified even to look at. The only occasion I'd spent real time away from President House before was during my stay in Barts Hospital; it just didn't make sense to me that I was forced to share cells with guys who'd committed much more serious crimes than me.

The routine and environment quickly became familiar, but that didn't make the place any easier to live in. The constant smell of disinfectant never left my nostrils, and I couldn't get used to the food because it was all absolutely disgusting. If you got boiled potatoes the chances were, out of the four you were given, two would be edible and the other two would be as hard as house bricks. We were fed three times a day, but I never felt like eating because I didn't do enough during the day to work up an appetite.

The days passed really slowly. There was no TV and the cell was bare. All we had for entertainment was an AM radio, which I'd asked Dot to send me in the post, or library books. As I've said before, I was a late starter at school when it came to reading. I only learned to read when I was ten years old, when the headmaster at Morland Primary got a grip on me and five other kids who'd fallen behind in the system. He kept us back from 3 to 4.30 p.m. every night, teaching us in his study. I became an avid reader in prison, picking up any books available, and was able to enjoy countless war stories and dozens of auto-biographies too.

I never once picked up a pencil or a pen to draw while I was in Feltham. It didn't even occur to me. Doing time sucks the life out of you, and I didn't have an ounce of creative energy in my body.

I heard a nasty fight break out in the neighbouring cell one day, and I was worried for the lad who was in there, because his cellmate was a bloody big bruiser of a fella. I thought he'd be in rough shape, but when I saw him in the dinner queue later on, without a mark on him, I was pretty shocked, not to mention relieved. I asked around and found out from another inmate what had gone on.

'A screw wanted the big fella's Rolex,' he explained. 'The young lad got it for him, in return for back-up and fifty quid's worth of puff.'

I didn't see the big guy at dinner that night. Supposedly he was in the medical unit. You could get hold of cannabis inside if you knew how, but I'd decided not to make my life any more complicated than it already was, and I was giving cannabis a rest, which wasn't difficult once I got used to it. Still, I can remember being surprised to find out that it was actually some of the screws themselves who were the cannabis suppliers, which shows you how naive I was back then.

One of my cellmates was a Spanish guy who spoke broken English, and seemed decent enough when I first met him. That didn't mean a thing though. I was learning fast that anything is possible in prison, and you shouldn't take anything or anybody at face value.

'What are you in for?' he asked me first.

'Deception. Six months for using stolen post office savings books.'

He looked relieved but a bit suspicious.

'You sure? That all?'

'Yes, I know. How 'bout you?'

I was wary of being spun a line, but this guy didn't hold back and seemed quite proud of his crime. He showed me his charge sheet, which was the only way you could be sure somebody was telling the truth, and it said he'd been done for blowing somebody up in an ETA terrorist attack.

'That's a new one on me,' I said, trying not to show my shock, and that was the end of the conversation.

We talked about all sorts of other stuff as the days rolled by; music, books, and what we might do when we got out. He was actually really good company and I was happier to share a cell with him than with somebody who was in for a random stabbing or assault, as so many of the other inmates were. I felt safe with him, as long as I didn't discuss Basque independence in any way, shape or form, which funnily enough, I didn't feel like doing.

On many a night you'd hear a disturbance along the corridor and find out the next day that some poor kid had tried to slash his wrists or hang himself, or had been beaten black and blue by his cellmate. I never slept well; I think I'd have felt more at ease kipping in the middle of the lion's den in London Zoo than in that place.

I was taken away in another sweat box to finish my sentence at Rochester prison in Kent, a far worse place than Feltham, which I'd really rather not talk about. I've got bad memories of that place. When I finally handed back my prison clothes and smelly socks, I thought to myself: 'I never want to be in trouble with the law again. And I mean ever, ever again.'

In that respect, my sentence had served its purpose, or so it seemed. I was adamant I was going to stay on the straight and narrow and never see the inside of another prison for as long as I lived. I walked out into the sunshine in the summer of 1990 feeling very grateful for my freedom indeed, and looking forward to starting the rest of my life.

Chapter Eleven

I look at George sometimes and wish I were a dog. He sits there without a care in the world, scratching his balls and looking at me wryly, as if to say: 'Hard life, isn't it, you mug.'

Meanwhile, I'm drawing picture after picture, working on commissions and new projects, writing this book and preparing for my next exhibition.

'You don't know the meaning of a hard life,' I say to George, who never once takes his eyes off me. It's the most incredible thing how he never stops looking me dead straight in the eyes. As if he's guarding precious cargo. There is a look of concern there, as if he thinks I am about to break.

He knows I don't mean that he's had it easy, because in time I did learn more about George and it turned out his past was as troubled as mine.

We lived in that bedsit on Royal Mint Street for nine months together, and each day I spent with him, he'd impress me with something new. I wanted to make sure he would never run into the roads or chase after cats again so I continued training him during our long walks. He was a natural and one particular incident gave me encouragement to push him even harder. We'd been going out for walks without George's lead for a few weeks. It wasn't ideal, but with my ankle I really struggled to keep hold of him and balance on my crutches, so in the end I left the chain at home. We had just left the flat and George was walking a few yards out ahead of me. As we turned the corner a couple of community support officers stopped us. They didn't look pleased. 'Sir, you have to keep that dog on a lead,' one of them said sternly. 'He's too dangerous to be loose. If he can't be off the lead, we'll have to take the dog away. Understood?'

I understood, but I didn't have much choice. I couldn't walk and keep George on the leash at the same time. It was impossible.

The next day we went out, I was keeping a close watch for the officers, keeping George as close to me as possible, but as soon as we got near the local park George sprinted off, as he always did. Just then, a way down the street and through an underpass, I saw the bright yellow hi-vis jacket and knew I was in trouble. They were walking towards us and I was sure George would be taken away from me. I hadn't seen where he had run off to and I was panicking wildly, calling his name as loudly as I dared. I felt something soft brush my leg and realised George had sidled up to me and was walking as closely alongside me as he could. I didn't see where he'd come from and I'm sure he can't have heard me calling, but it was as if he knew to come back to me right at that moment. Our steps were suddenly in sync and with the way my crutches were hanging it almost looked like he was on a lead! As we passed them I gave them a little nod, and a 'good day'. The minute we were past them and they were out of sight, George sprinted off again, legging it towards the park. All I could see was his tongue hanging out as he gained speed.

After this I upped the training, turning it into a game. The first lesson was to teach him him to sit on a kerb and make him stay until I gave the word. He was still very fidgety and restless, and as we were spending more time on the street together, I needed him to be able to sit and stay sat. If he moved a muscle without me telling him to, I'd bang my crutch on the floor and give him my mad voice so he remembered what happened when he misbehaved. Once I got him under control, I decided to test it. I took him to a set of traffic lights and told him to sit on the kerb. When I told him to move in my normal voice, he walked with me. As we got to the island in the middle of the road, I gave him my new orders to sit firmly. We repeated this ten times going backwards and forwards, crossing the road at the same set of traffic lights. Whatever the bystanders thought of us didn't bother me in the slightest. George was a bloody fast learner, and he seemed to be really engaging, as if he wanted to listen and learn.

The discipline I showed him was starting to pay off, and before long, his true character was shining through. Gone was the timid, shy, nervy little George. Here was a proud animal with electric energy and boundless bright eyes. His happiness was my happiness.

One day I was at Tower Gateway when a young policeman came up to me and started reading me the riot act. That's one of the occupational hazards of begging on the street. You're not meant to do it and, even though a lot of policemen just ask you to move on rather than take things further, you always get the odd one who threatens you with a dispersal order if you don't move along. Right away, George started growling at the young copper and giving him the evils. 'Bleeding jobsworth,' I was thinking.

'You took the words right out of my mouth' the look in George's eye said to me. The policeman eventually went on his way, my promises not to return ringing in his ears, and I gave George a gentle smack on the backside.

'Just one smack for being good. You'll get two tomorrow, if you're bad.'

I had to teach him not to growl like that at people, particularly policemen, but at the same time I was really pleased he'd behaved that way. It showed me he was feeling settled enough with me to want to protect me.

On Thursday and Friday evenings I started standing on Bishopgate with George, next to a pub called Dirty Dicks. It was really lively and busy, but by now George was an asset, not a hindrance in crowds of people. He'd stand as still as anything, even when the police dogs from Bishopsgate went past. Commuters would ask me if they could stroke him, and nine times out of ten they'd be the ones starting the conversation, which made the task of begging a lot more enjoyable.

'Where did you get him?' people would ask, stroking his round face. 'How long have you had him? What's his name?'

I'd chat away happily to them, and they always gave me a few bob before saying goodbye. They made a point of saying it was for George but I didn't care, it was for us.

Several months later I was begging outside a petrol station in the East End with George sitting beside me. He was very well trained by then and I only had to raise my voice and growl 'George. Don't you DARE' to have him stay obediently by my side. He was listening to my every command by now.

'Here, mate, is that George?' I heard a voice say. It was a slurred Scottish voice. Even though I'd never heard it before, the voice was somehow familiar, and I was immediately on my guard, taking tight hold of George's collar.

'That used to be my dog. Any chance of having him back?'

I couldn't believe my ears.

'Say that again, pal.'

'I said that's George and he used to be my dog . . .'

'You ain't getting the dog back.' I said, interrupting him. 'You sold him for the price of a can of lager, remember? So do me a favour and piss off!'

I was giving him my best hard bastard look, the kind of thing I'd seen all the time in prison, and I was careful that my voice didn't crack. I sensed we were in trouble.

This time he went straight to George. 'George, boy, d'you recognise me? D'you recognise your old dad? You'll have to come and stay with old Uncle Chick for a couple of days.'

I was boiling with rage but I tried to keep myself in check.

'That won't be happening, mate. He's my dog now. You sold him, now piss off and don't bother coming back.'

But George didn't react to 'old Uncle Chick' at all. He sat still, just the way I'd trained him to. He even looked a little bored. It was hard to work out what he was thinking.

'He remembers me,' the Scot said, sounding a little desperate. 'Look at him, he remembers his old dad, don't you, George?'

'He's just well trained now, that's all,' I said. 'He's my dog now, mate, and I've taught him how to behave. Now do yourself a favour and disappear. Do you hear? I never want to see your face again.'

'Aye, understood, pal,' he said finally, but I didn't trust him.

Shortly after our run-in, I heard on the street that the Scot was going to try and steal my George from me. When I heard that, I felt sick to my very core. The thought of losing him was too much to bear. I was keeping my eyes peeled for the Scot all the time. Whenever we'd go for walks I'd keep George close by and I always looked round to see who was behind me. I'm the sort of person who dwells on things, and I'd wake up in wild panics, thinking George had been taken. When I saw that he was sleeping in the crook of my leg or crashed out by my feet I'd feel like I'd won the lottery. By this point, I was completely attached to him, and I couldn't imagine life without him.

'You're alright with me, son,' I'd tell him. 'I'll look after you.' I would protect George until the end of the earth; that's how I felt.

I made a promise to George that the next time I saw old Chick I'd make it the last. It wasn't long before my promise had to be kept.

We were sat on our spot near Tower Hill tube station one afternoon when he sidled up to us. 'How's old George doing today?' he began. I wasn't having any of it.

'Listen to me and listen good. I've got a baseball bat with your name on it, written lengthways, sideways, back to front and upside down. If I ever see you again I'll use it. Know what I mean or do I need to show it to you?'

'Alright mate . . .'

'Do you understand very clearly what I'm saying?' I said, more camly then I felt.

'Alright mate, dog's yours . . .'

And after scratching George under the chin, off he went. Thankfully, we never heard of old Uncle Chick again.

As I write this one thing still puzzles me and that's how George reacted to him. If you didn't know any better, you'd think he'd had an easy ride in life. In my heart, I just knew that George wasn't that lucky, that he'd had a tough time somewhere along the line. I had to wait several more months before I found out the truth about

George's past. Walking down Columbia Road one day, this guy stopped when he saw us outside one of the shops.

He looked like he recognised George.

'I'll bet his name's George.' He said holding out his hand to me. 'And I'm Fred, by the way. Pleased to meet you.'

George didn't do anything that told me he recognised him, but Fred seemed nice and in no way threatening. I wanted to hear more.

'I bred George,' Fred explained. 'He sired a litter of puppies, but the bitch wouldn't let him near them. Every time he went close she attacked him, and that's how he got that nick in his ear.'

I knew Fred was a hundred per cent genuine now, because the nick in George's ear isn't very visible, and you wouldn't know it was there unless you really looked for it. It was exciting to learn more about George. He'd done so much for me and yet I felt like he knew me better than I knew him. At the same time I could feel myself getting anxious, mainly in case Fred was going to try to claim him back. He went on to explain that his daughter wanted a puppy, but he didn't want to give one to her of George's litter, as she had a drug problem and he knew she'd only sell the dog for drug money. He gave her George instead, because the bitch was giving him such a hard time.

'What happened after that?' I asked.

'I don't know. I've had two other Staffies in my time who have gone off chasing foxes and never come back, but I don't think that's what happened with George. One day I went up to my daughter's house and he was missing, but she didn't have a good enough explanation about what had happened. I could only guess that she sold him to feed her drug habit.'

It explained so much about George, why he was so twitchy in the beginning, and why he'd become so loyal to me when I started to train him properly. As far as I now knew, he'd had at least three owners before Becky and Sam, none of whom treated him the way he should be treated. Any dog forms a tight bond with whoever is looking after them, and if that keeps being broken it's very tough, especially for a young dog like George. When they're not trained either, and don't know what the rules are, that causes extra insecurity.

So, however much I tease George today about being a lazy, good-for-nothing bastard who's living the life of Riley, I say it with a touch of irony. He'd had a tough early life. We both knew what it was like to be lonely, rejected and unsettled, and I think we understood each other.

'So do you want him back?' I asked Fred with a lump in my throat.

I felt he'd been very honest with me and I had to know what he was thinking now.

'Nah, wouldn't dream of it, mate. He looks well. He's well trained and well fed. You keep him. You deserve him.'

'Am I glad to hear that!' I said. 'He's the only thing I have ever loved.'

'Soppy git,' came the reply – not from Fred, but from George, who was looking at me like I'd taken leave of my senses.

Chapter Twelve

'You can't come back here,' Gerry said.

He was staring me straight in the eye, like he really meant business. I had walked out of prison with a small carrier bag of belongings and taken a train straight to President House. I knew Dot and Gerry wouldn't exactly be hanging out the bunting, but I had definitely not been expecting to be turned away flat like this. Between them they had visited me on several occasions during my time away, and never once had they told me I wouldn't be welcome back.

'Is Mum there?' I said, panic rising in my chest.

'Dorothy! It's John at the door.'

Gerry stood blocking the street door, making it clear I was not stepping foot inside, and Dot appeared behind him, looking a bit flustered and wringing her hands on her apron nervously. I knew in that moment she was going to stand by Gerry. I felt my blood run cold.

I'm sorry, John, but your dad is right, you can't stay here anymore. It's just not possible . . .'

Dot looked devastated and even Gerry looked a bit shaken behind his steely glare.

'Well, what am I meant to do? I have nowhere else to go.'

'You should have bloody well thought of that before you got yourself nicked,' Gerry snarled. 'You can't say I didn't warn you enough times. How many times have I told you you'd be out on your ear if you didn't sort yourself out?'

'You fat twat,' I blurted out.

I'd never called him that before, and he was livid. 'Fuck off and never come back you ungrateful bastard.'

A couple of the neighbours heard the commotion and came out on the landing to see what was happening. Poor Dot didn't know what to do. I didn't want to make this any harder for her than it already was.

'Ok, if that's how you want it,' I snapped. 'I'll see you around.'

I turned and walked away and heard the street door slam behind me. My throat tightened so much it felt like somebody was throttling me. I was in tears as I walked along the passageway and down the stairs, away from my childhood home.

I needed somewhere to stay for the night. I thought about asking Jackie, Malcom or David, but all my instincts told me to leave them well out of this. They were all married now and had stable, happy lives. I'd caused them enough aggravation to last a lifetime already, and turning up on their doorstep asking for a bed for the night would have really been taking the piss. As for knocking on my friends' doors, I just didn't want to. As I've said before, I hadn't been brought up to go cap in hand to other people.

I walked around the estate in a daze for a while and then got on the first bus I saw, which happened to be heading towards the West End. I sat on the bottom deck, crying my eyes out, not caring who was looking at me. An old lady heard me snivelling and gave me a sympathetic look, which just made me feel worse. I sobbed like a baby in front of everyone on the packed bus. I didn't look where I was going and ignored all the stops, because I had no destination in mind. It began to dawn on me that I was homeless. It hit me hard on that journey. I was nineteen years old, fresh out of prison, and I was fucking homeless.

I jumped on the next bus, went in the opposite direction and got off at King's Cross, because I'd seen a lot of homeless people hanging around there. I had no plan; I just felt as lonely as hell and wanted to have some contact with other human beings. Some fella saw the state I was in and came over to talk to me. 'How old are you?' he asked. When I told him I was nineteen he said I should go to a place called Alone in London, which was on Pentonville Road and catered especially for teenagers like me.

'I'll take you up there if you like.'

'I can get there myself,' I said.

'I don't mind showing you the way. Got nothing else to do.'

I decided he was genuine; my time inside had given me a very good eye for spotting dodgy geezers and he wasn't one of them. He was just trying to make himself useful to a person in need, which is the way a lot of homeless people behave. They know what it's like to be at rock bottom.

The words on Alone in London's sign were written in blue on a black background that was dotted with stars and moons. Just looking at it made me feel depressed.

'Alright mate, you can leave me here,' I said to the bloke. 'Thanks a lot for your trouble,'

'No problem. Good luck, son. Things'll get better,' he said as we parted.

Standing outside alone, I found myself unable to put one foot in front of the other. I just couldn't go inside; I wasn't that desperate, not yet. There had to be a better option.

I swallowed my pride and ended up staying at a couple of friends' houses for a week or so. I think I made out that I was going back to President House once Gerry had calmed down, although I knew that wasn't going to happen. I didn't want to admit how hard I had fallen to anybody, even myself.

I might have been homeless that first night, but it wasn't permanent, and I didn't have to go around with a sign on my head telling everybody what had happened. I could turn this around pretty quickly – that's what I told myself, and that's what I wanted to believe. I could get a job and then find a place of my own. That was my plan.

A few days later I went round to Jimmy Dolan's and asked him for some work, because he'd been good to me in the past and I thought that was the best place to start. When Jimmy saw the state of me, I had to admit that Gerry had thrown me out, and I told him the whole story about me sleeping on friends' floors and sofas. Jimmy offered to not only give me work in the furniture shop but help find me some accommodation too.

'You know I'd take you in, John, but it's not really on, what with the family and all that...' he said. I was grateful that had even entered his head. He had a wife and children who barely knew me, and I would never have expected to put upon his family like that.

Jimmy drove me over to the homeless charity, Centrepoint, which was on Shaftesbury Avenue. We climbed an old wrought-iron staircase that was caked in bird shit and smelled bloody rotten. I walked through the door and into an open-plan room. There were a few sofas, an old TV and tea-making facilities, and lads scattered all around, just chatting and playing chess or cards. It shocked me to see how relaxed and happy they looked; I couldn't have been more devastated to be there.

Jimmy told me before he left that Centrepoint would only be for one night, two at the most. We'd go to Islington Council in the morning, and he was sure that once we had explained the situation we'd be provided with the necessary help.

On the first night in Centrepoint, I cried in front of everyone. That's my abiding memory. I remember lying in a little single bed, wishing I could be back at home, playing with Butch or watching TV, just doing normal stuff. It didn't feel real being in that place, even after my time in Feltham. It felt as if it was happening to someone else.

Jimmy took me out in his car the next day and the one after, and we ended up driving around all kinds of housing offices, being given the run-around. Eventually, after queuing up for hours in one place, I was given the address of a B&B in King's Cross, where the council would pay for me to stay on a temporary basis.

'Can he go on the list for a council house?' Jimmy asked.

The woman behind the desk practically laughed in our faces.

Me and Jackie (on the right), with one of Jackie's mates.

Jackie looking after her baby brother.

Me, aged five, sitting under the living room window in President's House.

From left to right: my brothers Malcolm and David,
my sister Jackie, Dot, my uncle Danny, Danny's girlfriend and Gerry.

John Button, my future brother-in-
law, and me, aged about ten.

Opposite: Looking a bit
nervous as a thirteen-year-
old in my school clothes.

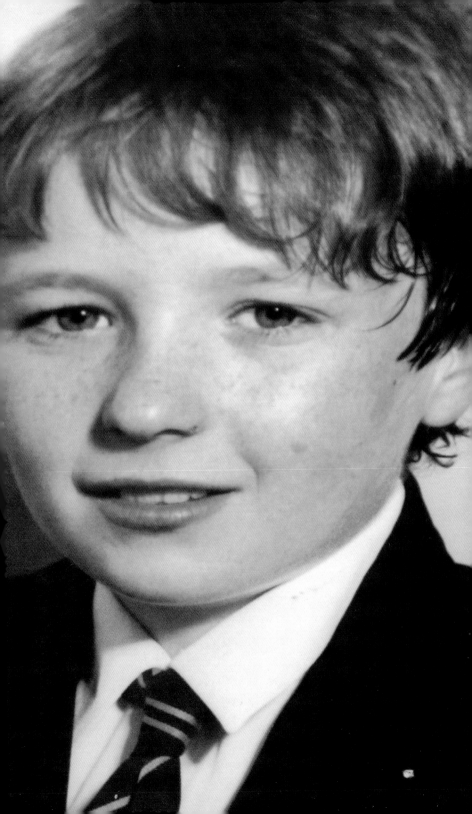

Above: Walking down Bethnal Green Road, trying to keep up with George.

Above left: Sat on Shoreditch High Street in the early days.

Me and George sharing a little smile.

Opposite top: At home with George. Bit messy but it's better than the street!

Opposite bottom: Having a time out on a park bench with George keeping me company.

Off to the office. The board is what I used as backing for my drawings.

Above: Another day on the High Street, with George out front with his cup and me drawing away.

Opposite: A typical Shoreditch High Street drawing with a little message in the billboard.

A note George wrote for passers-by at the
Columbia Road flower market. He's got good handwriting.

George the Dog. Shoreditch London.

Left: My first proper drawing of George. Really proud of this one.

Below: One of the last days I spent with my good friend Les.

Opposite top: My tribute to Stik. A drawing of Rivington Street which has some of his artwork on the wall.

Oppostite bottom: Shoreditch from the air. I drew this from the top of Broadgate Tower.

Top: Thierry Noir working on the collab.

Above left: ROA showing me the ropes. George has got his eyes on the sandwich he has his right hand. Greedy bastard.

Above right: Me, George and Stik, celebrating the completion of my drawing.

Top: A ROA mural in Bethnal Green. I love his stuff.
Above: A detail of the collab done by Thierry Noir and ROA.

Top: Sever's collab.
Above: Rowdy's collab.

Top: Cityzen Kane's collab.
Above: Stik's collab.

George posing in front of the Broken Fingaz crew collab.

Griff mucking in on the day of the opening, hanging some drawings.

George guarding the priceless works of art at the exhibition before the doors opened.

The queue builds outside the gallery. Getting close to opening.

Taking in the plaudits with
Stik and George.

Top: Checking out my handiwork
in my best artist's pose.

Above: The exhibition was
packed and turned out to be a
bigger success than I ever could
have imagined.

'He can, but the waiting list is seven years. That's unless he gets pregnant,' she said, attempting a joke. 'Then he can jump the queue.' Neither of us laughed.

The B&B was in the arc of King's Cross's red-light district and was an absolute shithole, but I told myself, and Jimmy, that it wouldn't be for long, and I'd soon sort out something better. There were cockroaches in the bathroom, which was shared with seven other people, and my roommate was a forty-year-old who stank of sweat. It wasn't paradise.

I soon found out that the people who ran the so-called 'hotel' were by far the worst part of the whole experience. Landlords like them were paid hundreds of pounds a week by the council for each person they put up, so they were raking it in. Nevertheless, their 'guests' were treated like the scum of the earth, house rules were laid down with a rod of iron, and they'd come up with every trick in the book to try to con every last penny out of you. One Greek–Cypriot landlady I had the misfortune to meet lined up ten of us guests like we were in front of a firing squad at breakfast one morning. She then walked down the row of us, addressing each person individually.

'You pay me poll tax!' she demanded, even though she had no right to ask for extra money, as the rent the council paid her included the charge.

We all argued until we were blue in the face, but she kicked out everybody who didn't cough up, me included. It was a similar story in plenty of other B&Bs, and unfortunately I stayed in a long list of shitholes during this period of my life.

Even if the landlords weren't completely tyrannical you'd always be booted out on your ear at 10 a.m. each morning, usually after having a greasy egg and a rubber sausage thrown at you. Typically you weren't allowed to return until 8 p.m., which is a bloody long time to fill. Most days I'd go and do some work for Jimmy, but he didn't need me full-time. He'd always give me a few quid, whatever he had on him, but a lot of the time I'd spend half the day sitting around smoking weed. I was back on it by then, and I'd be happy to let the hours drift by.

If I wasn't working for Jimmy I'd look for other ways to entertain myself. As I knew from my days of bunking off school, it's not easy to keep yourself busy on the streets all day with precious little money in your pocket. I'd sometimes buy a daily travel card and go round and round on the Circle Line, just watching the world go by. Or I might go to the British Museum and wander around the exhibits. Anything really. There were days I'd jump on a bus and go up to Parliament Hill Fields, where I would just sit for hours on the benches, thinking about how my life had got to this point.

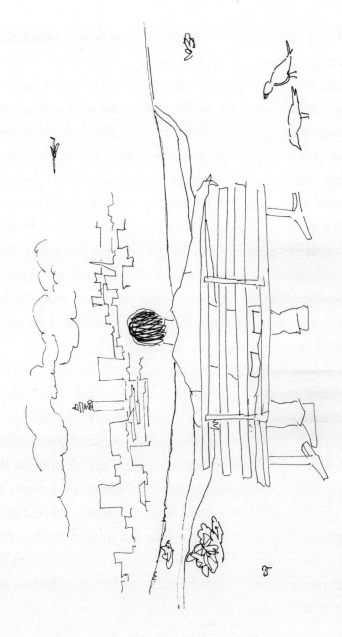

There's a lovely view of London from Parliament Hill Fields. I'd sit there for hours with my thoughts.

It was an incredibly lonely time in my life. I plucked up the courage to go and visit Dot and Gerry one day, about three months after I'd last seen them. I was still as mad as hell with Gerry for kicking me out, but I didn't want to lose touch with them completely; that would have been too much to bear on top of everything else.

'It's OK, I'm only visiting,' I said when Dot answered the door. 'You can tell the old bastard I'm not staying.'

She let me in, told me she was glad to see me and asked me what I'd been up to. Gerry gave me the time of day, but only just. I put on a brave face, telling them all about my job in Jimmy's furniture shop, and explaining that I had a roof over my head. I don't think I went into detail or explained that the roof kept changing and I was very far from being settled.

'I'm glad you've got somewhere,' Dot said. 'I've cleared your room out, by the way. Didn't really keep anything because none of the clothes would have fitted you. Have a look if you like.' I didn't bother. What was the point? Even if Dot had kept something I wanted – like some of my childhood drawings – I wasn't going to start lugging a load of my old crap in a backpack around London.

––––––––––

Both my mum and dad's health had started to fail by this time, which was another reason I didn't want to stay away too long. Dot had been diagnosed with cancer several years earlier, although she'd done a very good job of playing it down to begin with, and for a long time had never appeared to be ill. She had what was referred to in the family as trouble 'downstairs', which meant ovarian cancer. She never really talked about it and didn't discuss her treatment; either that or I had been too young to realise what she was going through when she was first diagnosed. Anyhow, she was now in and out of hospital, and for the first time she actually looked really ill. Her face was drawn and she was a lot thinner than the last time I'd seen her. It worried me.

'How's your health?' I asked her.

'Not bad,' she said. 'But not good either, John.' She looked me in the eye when she said that, wanting to get the message across. She didn't say any more, but it was obvious her condition was serious.

Gerry was also in a bad way. He'd developed asthma late in life and because his breathing had become so labored, he'd had to give up work. He was only in his late forties when he packed in his job, but from that point on he spent most of his time sitting at home just vegetating. He'd have the occasional bottle of cider or can of Guinness, but mostly he'd just sit on the sofa watching TV and drinking gallons of tea or big litre-sized bottles of Coke and lemonade. Practically the only time he went out was to medical appointments, and he wouldn't even take Butch out when there was nobody else around to do it. Gerry was one of those men who would never go to the doctor's until he absolutely had no choice, but David had seen him in a really bad state one day, coughing and wheezing, and had called an ambulance. It turned out one of Gerry's kidneys was damaged, and the dialysis treatment he was going through now had made him grumpier and more curmudgeonly than ever. When he looked at me I could see the resentment boiling in his eyes.

'We don't need no more trouble,' he warned me when I left the flat that day.

I didn't stay for long. It was a mild evening, and I went and sat on a bench in King Square park. When I looked around my old stomping ground, the days of the play lorry and Tin-Can Tommy were very fresh in my mind, but they also seemed so long ago. I was an adult now, out in the real world, and I was finding out how bloody hard life really was.

I didn't have the energy or motivation to go back to my latest B&B, and I lay down on the bench with my jacket under my head and eventually went to sleep. It wasn't very comfortable, but it was a clear night and at least I could look at the stars. Best of all, I didn't have some old harridan haranguing me or some smelly old man snoring in a bed next to me.

The next morning I didn't fancy the B&B at all. I decided sleeping rough was a better option, but I obviously didn't want to do it in my old neighbourhood. I didn't want my old friends to see me in this state. I'd already been to jail when they were all getting jobs or settling down with their girlfriends, and now I was homeless to boot. It was embarrassing and, apart from anything else, I just didn't think I'd be able to relate to my old mates anymore, because our lives had moved in such different directions. For most of the same reasons, I continued to stay away from Jackie and Malcolm and David. I'd already shown myself up as the wayward little brother; I would get back in touch with them when I was back on my feet and had something to be proud of, which I didn't think would be far off.

I went for a scout around later that day, looking for a place to sleep where I wouldn't be seen or found by anyone at all, and eventually I came across the perfect place. There was an old Volvo estate abandoned at the back end of a housing estate on Commercial Street, and I broke into it and stayed the night.

Just like on the park bench, it was a relief not to have to put up with the landlords I'd encountered in the B&Bs. The downside was that I didn't have breakfast to set me up for the day. The next morning I stole a sandwich from Safeway, and before long I was getting up early to see if I could nick food that was being delivered to local businesses.

There was a factory off Euston Road, near the Shaw Theatre, and I sussed out watching a few morning deliveries that they had their canteen food delivered at the crack of dawn. I'd nip down there just as the trolleys were being unloaded from vans and steal a pint of milk and a couple of croissants while the delivery boys had their backs turned. After a while, petty thieving became totally second nature to me. When my shoes started getting a bit knackered, I walked into M&S on Oxford Street and tried on a brand new pair. It was the only shop I knew of that had both the left and right shoe on display, and in those days they didn't have tags on. I walked out in the new shoes, leaving my battered old trainers behind. I did the same in Gap with jumpers and jackets, and then I'd go to McDonald's or Wimpy and spend the few quid I had in my pocket from working with Jimmy Dolan to buy a cup of tea. I'd stay as long as I could get away with before the staff would start giving me dirty looks, making it known I'd outstayed my welcome.

I slept in the Volvo for a few months until the winter was really setting in and I was starting to worry about freezing to death in my sleep. I'd acquired some blankets and coats, so I hung on there for as long as I could, because it still felt luxurious compared to the B&Bs. Weird though it sounds, I didn't want to give up the privacy. I'd met quite a few other homeless people at King's Cross station by now, because I'd go there when I was feeling lonely. Being with people who were in the same predicament as me always brought a touch of comfort. I can remember being in a cafe opposite King's Cross when a massive cheer went up all around the station one day.

'What's going on?' I said to a homeless guy I was sitting with.

'Don't know, mate. Let's find out.'

It was 23 November 1990, and we ran outside and were told Maggie Thatcher had resigned. I didn't see a single homeless person who wasn't celebrating that day. We all shared the same disdain for the Iron Lady. To people down on their luck she was the person who took money from the poor and gave it to the rich; we were all glad to see the back of her.

I still had a bit of work with Jimmy from time to time, but it wasn't enough for me to look after myself properly. I had no choice but to claim benefits, and it hurt. It was a real low point in my life. I was admitting defeat and acknowledging that I was failing to stand on my own two feet. I came from a family of grafters, and claiming help from the state was the last thing I ever wanted to do.

Five star service in the Volvo estate. If only!

A fellow homeless person told me about the Dock Street hostel, which was down by Tower Bridge, and with the winter coming on, and the Volvo getting colder and colder, I gave it a try. It was rough, but supposedly not as bad as the B&Bs up in King's Cross. It was a bloody big creepy-looking place with about three hundred rooms for men and women and in the past it had been used by sailors for about eighty years, when the docks were operational. There were two TV rooms, a big games room with a full-sized snooker table that seemed to get slashed with a knife every time it was repaired, and then there was a big dining area, which was the setting for many fights between the residents, and sometimes the staff.

I met some good people there, some strange ones and some mad ones. There was an African guy called Prince who used to tell residents that he was a real prince and that once he returned home he would be king of his nation or tribe – I can't remember which. And I remember that the head chef, Jeff the Chef, as we called him, had a very obvious hairpiece we all took the piss out of.

That's also where I met a lively guy called Legsy who was extremely entertaining, and very good company. He told me he lived with his mum on Commercial Road, but he liked hanging around the hostel. It didn't take long for me to notice that Legsy seemed to have a hell of a lot of disposable income for somebody without a job.

'What's your secret?' I asked when I'd got to know him a bit better.

'Commercial burglary,' he said with a wink.

'You serious?'

'Deadly. Wouldn't do none of that house breaking. Wouldn't wanna do that. But shops and cafes – very nice little earners. I can do £3K a night if I'm lucky.'

Legsy could tell a good story and I thought he was probably exaggerating; but there was no denying he had plenty of readies. Anyhow, the hostel was mostly full of people like me whose lives weren't going anywhere fast. Ninety-nine per cent of them were unemployed, many due to drink, drug or mental health problems. You didn't feel as unwelcome as in some of the places around King's Cross, but it was far from being a nice place to live.

Chapter Thirteen

'Mrs Ryan, can you come to the door on your knees with your hands on your head?'

It was just after 5 a.m. on 15 December 1991, two years after my arrest for the bank book deceptions. Dot was alone at the flat in President House as Gerry had been taken to hospital with kidney failure.

'Who is it? What's going on?' she called. She'd been woken up by the sound of hammering on the door and was half asleep and confused.

'It's the police. We need to talk to you. I repeat, Mrs Ryan, please come to the door on your knees with your hands on your head.'

'I can't,' Dot replied. 'I've got cancer. I'm in great pain.'

There was a pause, and then the officer shouted: 'OK, Mrs Ryan, put all your lights on and open the door.'

As she opened the street door into the freezing night air,

she noticed two armed police officers nearby, in the entrance of the public passageway in front of her. One was kneeling down, pointing a handgun in Dot's direction, whilst the other had a semi-automatic machine gun and was standing behind his partner, also training his firearm on Dot.

'What the . . . ?' Dot looked around in fright and shock as she stepped outside the door to see what was going on. That was a big mistake, because once she was outside on the balcony the door slammed behind her, and she wasn't let back inside. They told her they were there to search the flat but they had to wait for permission from someone high up at Scotland Yard before going in. In the meantime Dot was forced to stand on the balcony shivering and crying and frozen to the bone. The policemen stopped training their weapons directly on her when it was clear she was no threat, but they were still on alert and the situation was incredibly tense.

'Can't I just I go in and get something warmer to wear?' Dot begged the policeman who stood guarding her.

'I'm afraid not.'

'Then can't somebody pass me something warmer? I'm freezing to death here!'

'No, you'll just have to wait there until we've done our job.'

'What you looking for?'

'I can't give you that information.'

'Has this got anything to do with my son John?'

'I can't give you that information.'

It was a full hour before the police officers received the permission to go in and search the flat. Before they went in Dot told the police that Butch was in the flat alone, and was quite old.

'Please don't hurt the dog,' she begged.

The police took just five minutes to search the flat and establish that I wasn't there. Yes – it was me they were looking for, as per usual.

Once the police had left, Dot finally collapsed into bed, traumatised, freezing cold and clutching her stomach in agony. It later emerged that there had been an armed robbery in a newsagent in Smithfield, where the guy behind the counter had been pistol-whipped, and the police suspected I had been a part of it. They claimed that sniffer dogs at the scene had picked up my scent and led them to the flat. The only 'weapon' they found that day was a Derringer starting pistol I'd had since I was a kid. It had been on top of the fridge-freezer for so long it was covered in a thick film of dust.

The last time I'd seen her, I'd given Dot a phone number to reach me on if she needed to get hold of me urgently. That's how I came to hear about everything that had gone on at the President House that night.

'Don't come near the flat,' Dot told me. She was angry and upset, and even on the phone I could tell she was close to tears. 'Just stay away.'

'Whatever you want,' I promised her. 'I'll do what you say. I'm very, very sorry, Mum.'

Dot ended up in hospital two days later because she was suffering so badly with the pains in her stomach. Both she and Gerry were still in hospital weeks later, over Christmas. At the time I thought Gerry was the one who might not pull through, as he was now on dialysis full-time.

If I thought my reputation in the family couldn't sink any lower, I was wrong. My name was mud, not only with Gerry and Dot, but with my siblings too. Malcolm and David were blazing and refused to have anything to do with me, and even Jackie couldn't find a good word to say about me, however hard she might have tried.

As the New Year came around, the family was told by Dot's doctor that it was unlikely she'd be coming home again. Her cancer had become aggressive, and her health rapidly deteriorated over her time in hospital. The last time I saw her, I could barely keep it together. She looked so frail. Gone was the vivacious, lively woman I'd grown up with. One of the very last things she said to me was: 'John, you'll have to move back home to look after your dad.' She was thinking of others, right up to the end. A couple of days after that, she passed away. She was only fifty-two.

Her funeral was overwhelming. Three hundred mourners packed into the church, including friends and colleagues from all the places she had ever worked, old neighbours, and people from all over King Square. No one had an unkind word to say about Dot.

Soon after, I moved back into the flat. I'd been staying there for a short time before Dot passed away, mainly to look after Butch with Gerry still in hospital. It was strange being in the flat alone, seeing the chair Dot used to sit in and her apron still hanging on a peg in the kitchen. Although it was lovely to spend time walking Butch around the old estate, I didn't want to be there.

Gerry knew it was Dot's wish that I move back in to take care of him. He also knew he needed help and couldn't manage on his own. The alternative would have been for him to go into an old people's home, and he was too proud to let that happen. I thought it would be easy to take care of him. I thought wrong.

Gerry really gave up on life after Dot died. It must have been very hard for him to lose her. Even though weeks would pass when they wouldn't even talk to one another, they had come to depend on each other's company and they had forged a strong bond. Gerry missed Dot terribly.

After she passed, he would sit at home all day reading the papers and doing the crosswords. After that he would watch TV, read some books and have a cat-nap. For the previous twenty years Dot had done every-thing for him – all his errands, all the cooking, all the housework – and from the beginning, I inherited all of that. Nothing I did was ever good enough though, and he made it known every single day how much he resented having me there.

'What you doing here, you lazy bastard?' was the first thing he said to me every morning.

'Why you sleeping, you lazy bastard?' he'd say if I dared to shut my eye and have a snooze on the sofa.

'What's this shit?' he'd say, whatever I served him. 'Fucking useless! Can't even brew a decent cup of tea.'

It was exhausting and soul-crushing but after the way I'd left things with Dot, I didn't want to lose my relationship with Gerry and I persevered as much as I could. 'Why don't you come outside for a walk?' I'd say. 'Take Butch out with me?'

Butch was ten or eleven years old by then and had started to slow up himself.

'We'll take it easy. Just go round the block.'

'No, I'll have a panic attack,' he'd say.

'If you do we'll come back.'

'What if I faint?'

'You won't. I'll watch you.'

'You wouldn't have a fucking clue what to do! Useless bastard. Now fuck off and leave me alone. I'm not moving.'

The only fresh air he got was when he stood by an open window. The more he sat around and did nothing, the more his health deteriorated, and the more bitter and scathing he became. Malcolm, David and Jackie would turn up occasionally, bringing their kids round, and Gerry would always tell them what a useless, miserable bastard I was. By now Malcolm was married and had two daughters, Angel and Jessie, and a son called Jack. David was married too and had a daughter, Vicky, and two boys called Joe and John, while Jackie had two little girls called Natalie and Emily.

Malcolm and David would only just about manage to say hello to me when they called round. I don't blame them at all. It was very difficult for them to forgive me for what had happened to Dot. I was well and truly the black sheep of the family. I'd usually slink off to my bedroom whenever they turned up, because it was just easier for everybody if I kept out of the way.

I was still supporting myself with commercial burglaries, walking in and out of high-street stores with nicked goods.

Gerry knew what I was up to by now; you didn't need to be a genius to work it out with all the clothes and shoes scattered around the flat. Occasionally he'd ask me questions, as if he was genuinely interested, but he was unpredictable. I never knew if he was going to enjoy the story, which he did sometimes, or turn on me with a tirade of abuse for being a 'thieving little bastard.'

The opportunities to do more serious 'jobs' soon started presenting themselves, especially through my connection with Legsy, the guy I had met back at the Dock Street hostel. We'd been spending more and more time together and we'd been taking on jobs that would sometimes pay out as much as £5,000. We'd rob places like restaurants, tailors, warehouses; any place where they had dodgy security systems and where there was no chance of anyone getting hurt – apart from us. It was ridiculously easy, and it had become quite an addiction. The buzz of the break-in, the adrenalin that courses through your body, is like any drug – dangerous, and generally bad for your health. I came to see commercial burglary as a licence to print money, but in hindsight I really should have quit while I was ahead.

Legsy and I finally got caught robbing a Dunkin' Donuts shop near Embankment station, when a security guard in a building opposite saw us through the window and called the police. The first we knew of it was when the pitch-dark shop was flooded with the flashing blue light from the first police car that arrived on the scene.

Legsy had always drilled it into me that if we did get caught, I mustn't resist arrest. I had to put my hands on my head, and then hold them out for the handcuffs when I was told to do so.

'Be respectful,' Legsy had told me. 'You'll get bail if you behave. The desk sergeants couldn't give a fuck about commercial burglaries, but they will if you've given the arresting officer a hard time.'

I did exactly what Legsy had told me, because the very last thing I wanted was to go back to jail.

What a donut!

171

Chapter Fourteen

For the best part of my twenties, Pentonville Prison became my home. I was sent down after the Dunkin' Donuts robbery and then got myself into a spiral of criminality. I'd do three months inside, come out, commit more burglaries, get nicked again, then go back inside. It was a cycle I couldn't find my way out of.

With each stay in prison I would leave my dignity at the door as I went through the degrading routine of handing in my clothes and possessions. When I was shown my cell I had the same sick feeling in the pit of my stomach that I'd felt as a frightened eighteen-year-old at Feltham. It was like walking into a nightmare, knowing damn well you weren't going to wake up any time soon.

The trouble was, it wasn't greed or even wanting more of the finer things in life that had kept me going. The burglaries had become a way of life. I had nothing else going for me. I was still looking after Gerry, who was as angry as ever, and lonely after Dot's death. Going out with Legsy on our night-time raids made it all bearable. The excitement I felt on the jobs never left me. Every time I was looking for the money or a safe key in a cafe or a shop, I was buzzing. I loved that thrill, as well as the thought of sticking two fingers up to the police. It was never about the money.

Pentonville was on Caledonian Road, or the Cally, just up the road from where I grew up, and notorious for housing criminals of all types. There were murderers, rapists and all kinds – every crime you could think of had been committed by the inmates of Pentonville.

My first cellmate there was a big Irish guy who had the smelliest feet I'd ever encountered in my life. We had no television or radio, and every day felt like a week. He was on the top bunk, and he'd dangle his smelly feet over the edge of the bed and waft them around right by my face. I wanted to retch, but more than that I wanted to punch him right in the mouth.

The routine was mind-numbing but I guess that's how they wanted it, to give us plenty of time to think about what we had done. The cell door would be opened at 8.30 a.m. for twenty minutes, when you could go for a wander up the corridor, scrounge a fag or swap a magazine with another inmate. At 9 a.m., if you happened to be on what was called 'work detail', you'd be sent off to a prison workshop where you had to carry out frustratingly dull work, such as putting the sponge bits into those disposable headphones you get on flights. If you weren't working you had the option of education, if there was a vacancy on a course you wanted to do, such as computing or maths. Workshops were my saviour. I signed up for as many as I could. Prison life with nothing to do made me appreciate the window in Gerry's house. How at any time I could open it to smell the fresh air. Inside, we were offered no such luxury. I was stuck, not going anywhere any time soon.

I decided to clean myself up. I packed in the puff, which I'd smoked more or less daily since the last time I came out of prison, and tried to cut down on the fags, as I'd started smoking far too many; at least twenty a day. Gerry sent me £10 a week while I was in prison. He wasn't up for visiting which didn't surprise me, but I appreciated the gesture because he must have had a battle with himself over that, the way he despised me.

'I always said you were good for nothing,' he'd snarled when he found out I was going down. 'Useless piece of shit. How am I supposed to manage? You didn't think of that, did you?'

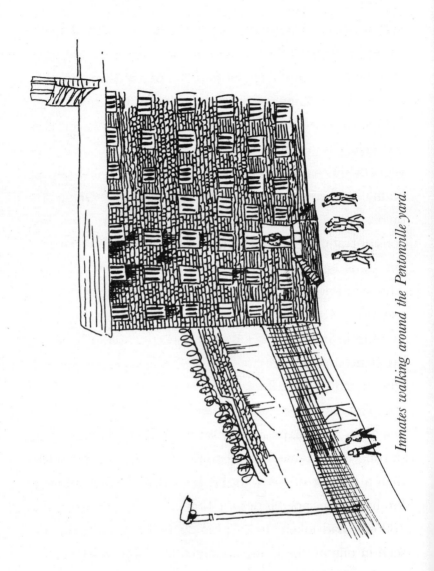

Inmates walking around the Pentonville yard.

It was true, I hadn't thought of that, because I really didn't think that I'd end up in prison. As it was, me going away and leaving Gerry to fend for himself was another big black mark against my name within the family.

One day we had two new drawing boards delivered to our cell. I had barely picked up a pencil or pen in five years by this point and I'd really let my art languish. It just hadn't seemed important with everything that was going on in life – my homelessness, Dot's death and Gerry's constant abuse – and in prison, nearly all your creative energy is banged out of you by the constant drudgery. This day, however, I was feeling a little more upbeat than usual and I picked up a pen and began to draw. I had nothing in mind when I started, but the pen felt good in my hand and the memories of my childhood fascination with comics came flooding back. It was like I was on autopilot and after a few minutes sketching, something had begun to take shape on the board. I kept pushing away, starting to lose myself in the creative process and in less than a quarter of an hour, I'd produced my first drawing for half a decade: it was a bareknuckle fight from the 1800s. I had taken the inspiration from an old print I'd seen in one of the library books a couple of days before: *Gin Lane* by William Hogarth. I remember looking down at the drawing and feeling like the two men in that fight.

Life for me was a big boxing match and I was losing, for now. There were still a few more rounds to go.

A screw called Mr O'Brien happened to be walking past the cell that day and my work caught his eye. He walked in and went right up to the board to have a good look at the picture. 'I like that,' he said admiringly. 'That's a really good drawing!'

His reaction took me by surprise, especially as you weren't allowed to stick anything on the walls.

'Thanks,' I said to Mr O'Brien. 'Haven't drawn nothing for years.'

As he was looking at what I'd drawn I could see a smile spread across his face, and I knew he genuinely liked it.

'Keep it,' I said to him. 'One day it'll be worth a lot of money!'

The drawing stayed on the board when I left the cell, and I never forgot that comment. It reignited my passion for my work and made me believe that I could still make it as an artist one day.

That day was still some way off as I had other, more pressing priorities in my life at the time. The first was surviving prison, then it was getting out, and finally, the tricky one, staying away from it. Those had become my only goals in life.

I knew next to nothing about hard drugs, until I was moved into a cell with a junkie called Tommy. When you arrived in prison you went cold turkey; there was no drug withdrawal unit in Pentonville at the time. We got talking, Tommy and me, and I guessed pretty quickly that he'd not had anything for weeks by the way he was trembling and sweating.

'Listen, can you help me out here, mate?' he begged me.

I was all ears; I'd have done anything so I didn't have to watch him suffer in that way.

'How can I help?'

'Will you cut me?' he asked pitifully.

'What you talking about?' I replied.

'If you cut my wrist for me, I can go to the hospital wing.'

'If you cut your own fucking wrist you can go to the hospital wing!'

'But I can't do it myself.'

'Why not?' I asked him. 'Why should I do it?'

He handed me his razor blade and wouldn't give up.

'Alright,' I said. 'But I'm only making a shallow cut. You're gonna have to hold still. No messing about now.'

He held out his arm and looked away while I attempted to make a long but minor incision in his arm. The idea was to create enough blood to get him taken to the hospital wing without doing him any serious damage. I pulled the razor blade lengthways on top of his forearm, from his elbow to the back of his wrist so as not to damage any veins. I hardly applied any pressure at all, and only just broke the surface of the skin, but suddenly Tommy's arm tore open like the lid of a can of beans under a tin opener. He was literally split to the bone.

We both screamed in horror, and in my shock I cut myself on my left hand, which started bleeding. Blood was pouring out of my cut a lot faster than Tommy's. His arm looked like something you'd see on a butcher's block, but there was barely any blood.

I found out later that his body reacted that way because he'd injected his arm so many times his skin was incredibly weak. Anyhow, forget the cold turkey; Tommy was now running around the cell screaming. I had to wrap his arm in a towel to calm him down as I banged on the cell door and called for help.

'This silly fucker's cut his arm,' I said when the screws came running.

Tommy was taken to an outside hospital because the cut was so deep. He claimed he had attempted suicide and was given fifty stitches. When he came back to jail a few weeks later, his eyes were glazed and he had a zombie look on his face, as the prison doctors were now filling him with heavy doses of Valium and antidepressants.

All Tommy had wanted to do was get high so I consoled myself with the fact I'd probably done him a favour in the long run.

———————

In between my sentences, life wasn't improving much. It was great to have my freedom back, of course, but returning to the flat always filled me with dread. Gerry's health had been getting steadily worse, and he was becoming more and more aggressive. Every time I went back, I knew I was in for even more of a kicking.

'What the fuck are you doing here?' Gerry would say. 'I don't need you, fucking waste of space. Fuck off!'

Sometimes I'd sleep all day and couldn't face leaving the flat. All my friends I had growing up had left and I didn't know anybody in the neighbourhood any longer. A lot of them had moved out of London but there were plenty, like me, who ended up in jail.

Butch was reaching the end of his life and I knew I was going to have to have him put down. The thought of it terrified me. Butch had been in my life since I was a ten-year-old kid and, even though I hadn't always been there for him, he'd been a constant and happy presence. I'd sometimes look at Butch, the way I do with George now, and imagine what he was thinking, or I'd tell him what was on my mind.

'Don't worry about him, he's a miserable bastard,' I'd say when Gerry had been kicking off and I'd taken Butch out of the flat for a breather. 'He don't mean it. He's a sick old man. Don't let it get to you.'

Butch would look me in the eye and I liked to think that at least he was my ally, even if nobody else in the family could stand the sight of me.

He was so old and ill that it was getting to the point where the kindest thing would be to put Butch down. When the day came to take him to the hospital, I had no cash for a cab so our final journey was on a bus. I carried Butch in my arms and sat down with him lying across my lap. I was dreading what was about to happen, and as the bus got closer to the pet hospital in Holloway I couldn't stop thinking about how I was going to be left alone with Gerry. I didn't know how I was going to cope without him.

My last memory of Butch is of the vet scooping him up awkwardly in the crook of his arm to take him away for his final injection. I could see that Butch was in pain, with his feet lifted off the floor and dangling awkwardly, and he took one long look at me before the vet turned his back and walked through the door. I stared back, taking one last look at my friend and companion of fourteen years. That was the last I saw of him. I'm certain he also knew that day was his last, and it was so painful for me that I couldn't bear to be with him when he took his last gasp. I'll be there for George when his time comes; I've already decided that. I just hope it will be many years in the future.

Saying goodbye to Butch was one of the saddest days of my life. I wasn't ready. My childhood pet had gone and with him it felt like another little part of me had died. I was twenty-four years old, I was alone, and I felt I had absolutely nothing left to live for.

I wandered out of the flat a few days later and went walking around some of the places I enjoyed visiting as a kid. Eventually I found myself on Brick Lane, thinking about going to all the famous London markets as a child, and all the stories I'd heard about the scams and the con artists over the years.

'Life doesn't stand still,' I thought, as I wandered the familiar streets. Even when you were doing nothing with it, like I was, it had a habit of drifting on and moving in directions you didn't see coming at all.

There was an Asian man standing on a street corner by a baby shop along Brick Lane, and I watched people going up to him. He was clearly selling drugs, and he kept them wrapped in pellets inside the cheeks of his mouth. Once he'd done a deal, he spat a pellet into his hand. They were made out of cut-up plastic bags you get in convenience stores, the ones with the red and blue stripes. The stripes were cut into little red and blue squares, and inside each square would be a scoop of drugs, tied up with a little knot at the end to stop the powder falling out. The red pellets contained crack cocaine, which is known as 'white' on the street, and the blue pellets contained heroin, which is known as 'brown'.

The drug dealer kept them in his mouth like that so that if the police turned up it would be easy to swallow them. I'd never seen a dealer doing anything like this before, and I went up to the bloke and said: 'What you selling?' He said he only had crack that day, and in the spur of the moment I bought twenty pellets. That set me back £300, which was every penny I had on me.

I'd snorted a bit of coke at a mate's house once and liked it, and I figured it was just what I needed to give myself a lift out of the depression I was feeling. I don't recall having any worries about what I was getting into, or whether I'd become addicted. All I could think of was how to stop myself feeling so down. It worked as I knew it would, giving me a high and letting me escape from reality for a bit, which was all I wanted.

About three months later, when I was having a particu-larly bad day with Gerry and my depression, I went back to the same bloke.

'Have you got any more crack?'

'No, mate, only got brown,' he said, meaning heroin.

I walked away at first, feeling not just disappointed but desperate. Why did he only have heroin? I'd always hated heroin since that day in prison with Tommy. Seeing how badly he wanted me to cut him, just to get some relief from his withdrawal symptoms, had left its mark on me.

Now I was wavering though, because I was so depressed. I had to have a chemical boost; that's how I felt. I could barely put one foot in front of the other to walk away from the dealer, and even just taking my next breath was bloody hard work because my heart felt so heavy. With my brain messed up with negative thoughts and intrusive voices, I talked myself into buying a £20 ball of heroin.

'It's a tiny amount,' I said to myself. 'I'll only smoke a bit. I've taken other drugs and not got addicted.' I was giving myself a running commentary, trying to justify what I knew was a stupid decision.

I put about £2 worth on tin foil, put a flame to it and smoked it. I knew what to do from being around users at King's Cross when I was homeless. The powder has to turn to resin, and when it runs down the foil you breathe in the fumes through a rolled-up tin-foil tube. Even when I was 'chasing the dragon', as this is called, I was thinking about how dangerous it could be, but I was so desperate for any sort of release from my depression that I didn't care.

I took a hit and a warm feeling radiated from my stomach and gave me a comforting glow around my whole body. It was instant, and it was like someone was giving me the biggest hug I'd ever had in my entire life. It was a totally different high to the crack. It was more of a relaxed, pulling back kind of a feeling, and I loved it. It didn't matter to me that it was a chemical hug, and a dangerous and addictive one at that; it was exactly what I craved. My depression lifted for the first time in what felt like years, and I heaved a huge sigh of relief.

Later on, I congratulated myself for taking a sensible amount. I didn't get addicted after that first smoke. All I felt was a bit lethargic and achy the next day, but nothing more. I thought I'd got away with it.

Gerry fell gravely ill in the winter of 1996 and died in January 1997. He went into hospital on the Monday and passed away on the Sunday, aged fifty-eight. Just prior to that he had stopped talking to me completely, and when he was admitted to hospital he had told everyone in the family that he didn't want to see me.

When I went to visit him on his ward at the Royal London in Whitechapel, a nurse stopped me and wouldn't let me in.

'Bollocks,' I said, pushing past her, and walked over to his bedside. Gerry had been drifting in and out of consciousness but he had heard the commotion I'd made.

He opened his eyes, looked at me and grunted: 'What are you doing here?'

Before I could reply, his sister appeared from behind me, grabbed my elbow and spun me around: 'Go on, John. You're not welcome,' she said.

I wasn't going to argue. 'OK, I understand,' I replied quietly. I didn't even look back at Gerry. That was it — the very last time I saw my dad alive. He was laid to rest next to Dot in the City of London cemetery; he had survived her by just five years.

———————

I had to move out of President House after Gerry's death, because it was a three-bedroom property and the council needed to put a family in there. I can't say I was upset to leave, even though it had been the only family home I ever lived in. Everything had changed. Memories of being a little boy, seeing my mum at the kitchen sink, or watching for my dad from the window, might as well have belonged to another world. All my childhood memories had been overshadowed by my troubles of recent years.

I was rehoused in a one-bed flat in Macclesfield House on Lever Street, but I managed to mess that up too. I lost it when I fell into rent arrears and failed to go to the repossession hearing, on account of me being in Pentonville on another short stretch.

Slowly but surely, my heroin use had increased. I went from smoking it once every three months, in increasing quantities, to using once a month, then once every three weeks, then two and so on. By the time I was twenty-eight years old, I had a twice-a-day habit.

In the beginning, each time I went back to it I was looking for the chemical hug I'd had that very first time. But it didn't matter how much or how frequently I chased the dragon, I never got that same feeling back. That's the dangerous thing about heroin. I didn't think I was addicted for a long time, but looking back I was hooked from the very first time, because I kept going back for more, looking for that warm glow. I wasn't enjoying it anymore, I was taking just enough to ward off the withdrawal symptoms. I needed more and more heroin just to feel normal and survive through the day.

I relied upon the burglaries more than ever now too. I wasn't just thieving to enjoy the experience of buying a new pair of shoes or a posh shirt any more. I now had an expensive drug habit that I needed to fund. Finding the money to pay for the heroin I craved took over my life. From the moment I woke up in the morning, that was my sole purpose in life.

That's the miserable state I was in for the best part of ten years, until I met George.

Chapter Fifteen

'How d'you fancy moving to Swanfield Street?'
George didn't look impressed

'Sounds crap,' his face said. 'Why you smiling about it?'

Ever since I'd been released from my last stretch in prison I'd been badgering the council to help find me a bigger place. My bedsit in Royal Mint Street was smaller than a prison cell and seemed to have shrunk in size since George had moved in. I don't think he'd got bigger in the nine months I'd had him, but he'd certainly grown in confidence, and he seemed to occupy a lot more space than he had in the beginning. George had soon become lord of the manor, trotting round as if he owned the place, stretching out on the sofa and having a big, energetic scratch whenever he felt like it.

'Shift!' I'd say every time I wanted to stretch out. He'd wrinkle his forehead and try to look hard done by when

I made him sit on the floor. Minutes later, after getting up and doing about ten laps of the bedsit, he'd be back, fighting for space on the sofa. 'Your turn to shift now, lazy git,' his face said.

Anyway, I had been offered a one-bedroom flat in Swanfield Street on the Boundary estate in the East End, which is one of the oldest council estates in Europe. I'd have taken a flat anywhere in London to get more space, and it was pure chance that this one came up in Shoreditch, which was very close to where I grew up, and was a place I knew well from my childhood.

When George and I moved into the flat it was the summer of 2010 and I had just turned 39. All I had were the clothes I stood up in and a can-opener for George's dog food. The flat was unfurnished, we were on bare floorboards and I didn't even have a cooker. I was given a grant of £200 to do the place up, and eventually I put in a carpet and bought a bed.

My benefits had been reduced to the point where they didn't really cover the rent, let alone food and bills or kitting the flat out. Begging alone clearly wasn't going to keep the wolf from the door.

'What are we gonna do?' I said to George. I was sitting on the hard floor next to him, trying to figure it out. 'Can't go out and get up to my old tricks now, can I?'

———————————

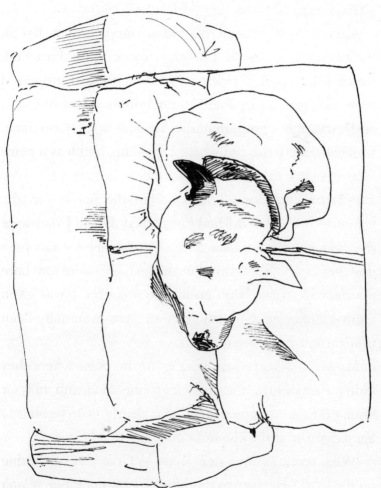

George asleep on the sofa.

By the time George had come into my life, I had more than three hundred convictions to my name and had been in prison over thirty times.

You might be thinking that I couldn't have been much of a thief to get caught so many times over the years, but the truth is I found it so hard to cope with life on the outside that I had started to effectively check myself in to prison for the winter. It got to the point where I wouldn't even bother to cover my tracks while I was out burgling. I'd deliberately not wear gloves so I'd leave fingerprints, or I wouldn't clean up after myself if I grazed my arm and started bleeding.

I knew what I was letting myself in for in jail, but at least inside I didn't have to worry about having a roof over my head and feeding myself, which was sometimes too difficult to deal with on the streets.

It's exhausting being homeless, shifting between day centres and hostels or missions, or sleeping in cars and bin sheds as I had to do after losing my flat in President House. Sometimes I was so desperate I felt like chucking a brick through a police station window and holding out my hands for the cuffs, just so I could get a bed for the night.

I was stuck in one such cycle the day George came into my life. He turned up after I'd been out of prison for about seven or eight months, and the cold winter of

2009 was really setting in. Under normal circumstances, I'd have been thinking about getting sloppy on the next job, so as to get myself a short stay inside that would tide me over until the weather warmed up.

As it was, George had his feet well and truly under the table by the time I got round to thinking about that, and that threw a bloody big spanner in the works. If I went to prison, I would lose George. It was as simple as that. We'd come too far for me to even consider that an option. For the first time in what seemed like an eternity, I had someone other than myself to care for, and it had filled my life with meaning. Over the years, I had met a few girls and I'd had a few relationships here and there, but nothing that had lasted more than a couple of months at most. I'd seen how my brothers and sister were with their children and how much love they had for them; I was beginning to feel that way about George.

My feelings for him became crystal clear to me one day when we were sat outside Fenchurch Street station and a well-to-do woman came up to us and started raving about George.

'What a lovely dog!' she said, scratching him on his head and generally making a big fuss of him. 'He's absolutely gorgeous! I've never see such a cute Staffie. I don't suppose you would let me buy him off you?'

I was completely stunned and totally speechless. Who was she to ask that?

'He's absolutely fantastic,' she continued. 'I'd give you a really good price . . .' She started to say she could pay £2,000 cash, but I stopped her in her tracks.

'Look, no offence, miss, but have you got kids?' I asked her.

'Yes, but I know Staffies and I'm sure he's good around children...'

'No, forget that. What I'm saying is, how would you feel if I asked you if I could buy one of your kids?'

She looked at me in confusion.

'You see the thing is, George is like my son. I love him like he's my own flesh and blood. I wouldn't sell him for two grand. I wouldn't even sell him for a hundred grand. He's too important to me.'

She was very gracious about having her offer turned down flat. There were no hard feelings and even George had a twinkle in his eye when the lady walked away.

Anyhow, that conversation had cemented what I already knew to be true; I was sticking with George come hell or high water. I just wasn't sure how I was going to do it, not in those early months. George meant a hell of a lot more to me than anything else in the world. I loved him, and losing him was unthinkable.

———————

George the Dog

Shoreditch, London

Sat together on the floor of my bedsit, I was remembering that woman and the crazy amount of money she'd offered for George. Two thousand pounds would have been mighty nice right then.

'I should have sold you to that lady, George. Could have got myself a nice gold watch for that.'

George let out a sigh, lay down and put his head between his front paws. He looked quite sad, to tell the truth, and I felt bad.

'Oi, listen, I was only joking. It ain't your fault,' I said. His ears pricked up.

'Well I suppose it is, you daft git,' I laughed, 'but that's a good thing, mate. Don't you worry.'

I thought back over the time I'd had George. I had barely let him out of my sight since the day I took him on. I wouldn't even leave him tied up outside Tesco if I needed a tin of dog food; I'd always ask a mate I trusted to keep an eye on him for a minute, and I'd dash in as quickly as I could.

To begin with I was terrified of the mad Scot showing up, and then after that lady tried to buy him, I was scared stiff of him being stolen.

Leaving George alone to go out thieving was completely out of the question. My gammy leg already made that difficult, because I wasn't as nimble as I used to be. What if I got caught and was put in the cells overnight? Who would feed the dog and take him out? I knew full well I would lose George for good if I got locked up, because there was nobody I knew who would be able to look after him for me for any length of time.

'That ain't happening,' I said out loud, thinking about being banged up again. 'I need to get a job.'

George was sitting up attentively now and had one of those looks on his face that said 'Silly bastard, how you gonna do that?' but I wanted him to know what was on my mind. I suppose I *was* a silly bastard to think he might have understood, but he seemed to be listening to me.

I know I was also a very stupid bastard for being nearly forty and having no job prospects whatsoever. Who would take me on with a criminal record as long as mine? It read like a telephone directory. And, even if some poor bugger was mad enough to take a chance on me, how would I manage to hold down a job with George by my side? It was beyond me.

There was only one thing for it. I didn't want to have to rely on begging for ever, but I knew I had to carry on doing it in the short term at least, or the pair of us would starve. It was that simple.

'Come on, George,' I said. 'Let's go and take a little stroll down Shoreditch High Street.'

Chapter Sixteen

Shoreditch High Street was a completely different place to the bland, grey, run-down road I remembered from my youth. The place was bustling with young and hip people who created a buzzing atmosphere. The view of the City, with the Broadgate Tower and all the other skyscrapers shimmering in the distance, made me realise just how quickly this part of London was changing. As George and I walked along together, the thing that struck me the most was how urban culture blended so easily with the corporate world. Just up the road from all these enormous skyscrapers, there were old industrial buildings covered in amazingly colourful murals, beautifully detailed and striking on the eye. I'd heard of Banksy – who hadn't? – and knew how much he'd done for raising the profile of street artists, but I had no idea street art had become so popular and widespread; the term wasn't even in my vocabulary. Being in an area where art was so present and so important to its identity made me feel right at home.

The sun was out and there was a buzz in the air, like the whole area was really alive and thriving. There were City boys in sharp suits coming out of bars, workmen caked in plaster dust eating sandwiches from the garage, girls in all sorts of bloody crazy fashions peering in shop windows, and loads of student types milling around.

I noticed an old man sitting begging on the pavement. He had a big quilted sleeping bag wrapped around his shoulders even though it was one of the rare warm days. Nobody seemed to turn a hair at this man's appearance, and I watched as people from all walks of life gave him a nod and a few bob. It was heart-warming. That first walk down the High Street took my breath away; I felt like I was stepping into a new world.

I took the bull by the horns and found myself and George a busy little spot by the Texaco petrol station at the end of the High Street nearest to the overground station. I was used to standing up and walking about when I asked commuters for change around the underground station at Tower Hill and on Liverpool Street, but here it felt much more relaxed, so I sat down on the pavement with George beside me.

I put a paper coffee cup in front of me and just sat there quietly for a while, soaking up the atmosphere and watching the world go by. People started putting money in the cup even without me asking, some made light conversation, commenting on how George was a lovely-looking dog or asking me for his name.

It's always easier to beg when the weather is warm because people don't walk so fast, and they're generally in a better mood, but I'd never thought it would be this easy. Shoreditch was obviously used to beggars and homeless people, so I started going back every day to the same spot.

We always earned enough for food for the day, and a little extra.

It felt good to get by without resorting to stealing but it still didn't change my thoughts about begging. I'd always hated it. With each penny I was given, I felt shame and embarrassment. I think the fact that I was doing it right on the doorstep of where I grew up, on the street I'd walked down with my family as a little boy, made it ten times worse. I would have died a thousand deaths if Jackie had walked past, or Malcolm or David for that matter. None of them lived very far from here, and the idea of them seeing me in this state preyed on my mind. I'd made a promise that I would only see them again when I'd sorted myself out. But at that moment I was still a bloody long way off achieving that. I didn't have a better plan, so I kept going back to the High Street, day after day. George and I survived on the kindness of others and for the time being that was good enough.

A few weeks later, I realised that it was better to sit on the opposite side of the road to the petrol station, because there was one of those green metal electricity boxes on the pavement I could prop myself up against. It was more comfortable sitting there when my arthritis was giving me gyp, and the view was better too. The City of London was to my left, and the old Victorian buildings across the High Street were in front of me. The juxtaposition was stunning.

I trained George to sit with the cup in front of him, as if he was the one who was begging. This served two purposes: it drew attention to us, so more people put money in the cup, and it also made me feel less sorry about my situation, because the cup wasn't directly in front of me. I could barely believe how far George had come. When I first met him as an unruly puppy. I couldn't have imagined I'd have him well-enough trained to sit still on a loud and busy street for hours at a time.

I was always thinking about how I was going to get off the street and make an honest living for myself and George. Seeing all the art around Shoreditch, I began to wonder whether I could make a few quid out of drawing something myself. Some of the street art I'd seen wasn't exactly fantastic, which encouraged me to think about using my own skills.

As you can imagine I wasn't exactly brimming with confidence. I hadn't drawn anything for many years and I had no idea how good I was now.

'Don't suppose you have to be Picasso to make a few bob,' I thought to myself. I was looking at George, thinking about feeding him and keeping him warm.

'What d'you think?'

'Just do it,' George said, or at least I reckoned that's what he would have said to me. 'Let's face it, what else have you got in the talent bank?'

'Nothing.'

'Then do it.'

'But what if I can't do it anymore? We'll be even further in the shit.'

'You won't know until you have a go. What have you got to lose?'

These kinds of thoughts ran through my head for days, if not weeks. I kept putting off having a go, but one day I was just so bored sitting on the pavement doing bugger-all that I started to sketch a section of one of the old buildings in front of me. As soon as I started to draw I felt excited. It came out of me effortlessly and the hustle and bustle around me seemed to quieten as I drew the details of the architecture. I felt positive, as if I had a purpose. I hadn't anticipated that, and it felt good not to be just sitting there doing nothing, waiting for people to put money in George's cup.

The sketch wasn't bad at all, and the next day I drew exactly the same building, because I wanted to improve on what I'd done the day before. It was 187 Shoreditch High Street, which used to be the old Leather & Suede shop. I'd only ever drawn faces and figures in the past, but the old buildings along this end of the High Street fascinated me. The more decrepit they were, the more interesting I thought they looked. I picked out the most dilapidated buildings I could find and started copying the minute details of the damaged brickwork and crumbling door frames and windowsills. I even drew the graffiti tags and street art which covered the rooftop.

Just having a pen in my hand and drawing again was a breath of fresh air and I absolutely loved not feeling like a beggar anymore. It was like saying to passers-by 'I'm an artist, looking for work,' rather than 'Can you spare some change?' I wasn't counting my chickens just yet, but my spirits were definitely a bit higher than they had been for a while.

The drawings I produced at first weren't perfect, but even on a bad day I could see that all I really needed was more practice. That's why I drew the same buildings over and over again; it's what's known as a 'study'. I wasn't planning to try to sell anything at this stage because none of the pictures were complete and I didn't think they were good enough, but I could feel I was getting somewhere.

Besides, I figured that even if I did produce saleable pictures of the buildings on the High Street, they wouldn't bring in much money. I began to think that the best way to make a decent amount of cash would be to teach myself how to do watercolour. Then I thought I could go up to Hampstead, draw some of the posh houses and try and sell my pictures to the wealthy homeowners.

'Wish me luck, mate,' I said to George every day when I settled down in front of the electricity box. 'Our future depends on this!'

George always had the cup in front of him and sat there very still. Every day he would look at the cup and then at my paper and pens, as if to say; 'About time you pulled your finger out.'

Then he'd sit there looking thoughtful, letting me get on with what I had to do.

As soon as I had enough money I bought some good-quality paper and fine-tip black pens from the art shop up the road. Over and over again, I'd practise drawing the filthy chimney stacks, the battered TV aerials, the graffiti tags, and the weeds growing from the tops of the build-ings, as well as sections of the buildings and all the tiny detail of the brickwork.

I ended up drawing the same two buildings – 187 and 189 Shoreditch High Street – literally two thousand times or more, trying to get the details just right. That probably sounds tedious, but it never felt like that. It wasn't like drawing a bowl of fruit over and over again. Even though I sat in exactly the same spot every day, my view of the street was never the same twice. Scaffolding and skips would come and go, shop fronts would change overnight and students in all sorts of fancy gear would stand around decorating the pavement.

The landscape was moving and evolving day by day. I'd watch the area developing before my eyes into a huge hub for street art and culture, and I wanted to capture the old Shoreditch before it was too late. I never drew the people; I was only interested in the old buildings, but the point is that the environment and the vibe on the street inspired me.

After a month or two I felt like I was getting somewhere and I started to feel like a proper artist, although I'd still have plenty of moments when I looked at what I'd drawn and think it was total crap.

'What d'you think?' I'd say to George when he looked over at me.

'Total crap,' he said, I swear.

I knew I needed to keep improving, but I also knew I was getting somewhere. I went out in all weathers, never missing a day. When it rained I wrapped black bin bags round me and George, and when the weather turned cold I got George an old daffel coat and wrapped him up in it. I'd put it on him back to front and wind the arms round his back so it wrapped him up like a snug blanket. He never complained; in fact he'd stand very still to make it as easy as possible for me to get it on him.

'Oi, mate, that's fucking cruel!' a drunk shouted one Friday night. He'd been to Brown's strip club down the road, and started telling me I should take George home.

'I think you should mind your own fucking business and take yourself home, mate,' I said.

I'd had a few less aggressive comments along the same lines. Women would say: 'Oooh, is he alright sat there in the cold?'

'Yes,' I'd tell them. 'If I tried to leave him at home he'd go mental. He loves it out here.'

It was true. The minute George heard me open the door of the flat each day he'd be on his feet. He was always more desperate to get out than I was. Whenever I did leave him alone indoors, he'd whine and moan.

'Look at you, you silly sod,' I'd say. 'I'm just going to the corner shop. I won't be gone ten minutes.'

'I know your ten minutes,' his expression always said.

One night, I was walking past the strip club on Hackney Road when I spotted one of the doormen standing outside, having a breather.

I did a double take when I saw him standing on the pavement. I knew his face well, but it took me a minute or two before I realised who he was. He was Mr O'Brien – one of my old screws from Pentonville! He was the bloke who'd seen my drawing of the bare-knuckle fight from the 1800s. I didn't think he'd recognise me now, or perhaps he might not want to recognise me, and so I didn't introduce myself on this occasion. But seeing him and remembering his compliment gave me a huge confidence boost.

'You know what, I'm gonna make it as an artist,' I said to George that night, because I was starting to have a very strong feeling that I would. 'I'm gonna be rich, you watch.'

George looked unimpressed, so I went on: 'And Brad Pitt's gonna play me in a Hollywood movie. It's a shame, though, as he's not as handsome as I am.'

I started to have a little daydream about getting back in touch with Malcolm and David too. I thought about all of my family often, and when I started to believe in myself becoming an artist I fantasised about telling them I'd finally sorted myself out and made them all proud.

The previous year, at the start of 2009, I was watching the local news on TV when I suddenly heard the presenter say: 'And also in the New Year's Honours list is postman David Ryan . . .'

I stopped in my tracks and watched the report. Blow me – my big brother David had been awarded an MBE for his services to the community! Even though he now worked as a postman, he continued to teach boxing at the Times Amateur Boxing Club three times a week and he had done a phenomenal amount of voluntary work, helping to keep kids off the streets. 'Yes, my mum would be very proud,' he told the reporter when he was questioned about his background, which made the hair on the back of my neck stand on end.

David was in his fifties and it was quite a shock to see him after all this time, but most of all it was inspiring. I was so proud of him, and I desperately wanted to be able to get back in touch and finally make the family proud of me too.

I carried on sitting on the pavement even when it snowed and my fingers went blue because I couldn't draw with gloves on. I didn't let the cold get to me, and even though my arthritis was killing me, I didn't stop. I had too much riding on this.

'It'll be worth it, you'll see,' I'd say to George.

'Better bloody had be,' he always seemed to reply, but he never complained, even when it was freezing cold, hailing or blowing a gale.

I eventually saved up enough money to get George a thicker coat, lined with sheepskin, and whatever the weather threw at us he sat on the pavement as good as gold, as if he'd been there all his life.

I felt accepted into the local community very quickly and began to enjoy sitting on the High Street, having the same people say hello to George and I everyday.

I knew a few of the homeless guys and other people begging around Shoreditch from various missions and hostels I'd stayed in over the years, and most of them were friendly to George and I.

Once I'd established myself as a regular on the street, they told me there was a rota for the position at the cashpoint outside Tesco, because that was the best spot in the whole of Shoreditch. I liked the way they all respected the unwritten rules of the street and took turns there. I didn't get involved in that because I was happy with my patch on the opposite side, and they all respected that too and left me to it.

TAKE MY PICTURE BY ALL MEANS...

When it was cold and George was wearing his sheep-skin coat, people started asking me if they could take his picture. 'Of course,' I'd say, hoping they'd put a coin in his cup by way of a thank you. Unfortunately, plenty of them took the picture and just walked off.

In the end I put up a handwritten note saying: 'Take my picture by all means but please put a coin in my cup other-wise I might bite you! Have a nice day, George the Dog.'

Most people saw me drawing and understood where I was coming from. I didn't have a sign in front of myself, but really I was saying to people: 'I'm an out-of-work artist.'

'I like the fact you're not asking for money,' people started to say. 'It's good that you're sitting there doing something.'

On Friday and Saturday nights, I got quite a few flash City boys coming out of the sports bar, and giving me £10 or £20 notes. If they did that I'd hand them one of my drawings, because it was only fair. The pictures were just studies and unfinished sketches at this stage because I was still practising, but at least they got something in return.

Once I got a couple of aggressive fellas shouting at me 'Oi, why don't you get a fucking job!' but I was prepared for that; I'd been expecting it.

For a while now I'd been training George to bark when I pointed my finger at somebody. He picked up the command really quickly, as he did with everything I taught him. If he barked when he shouldn't I'd raise my voice or give him a gentle smack on the arse with my hand, but when he barked after I pointed my finger I gave him a load of fuss, time and time again.

When the fellas had a go at me, I didn't say a word. I just lifted my arm and pointed at them, and George let rip, growling and barking and scaring the fellas half to death. They never troubled me again after that.

I'd also trained George to sit very still when he saw other dogs around. He never bothered with little dogs, but if he saw bigger ones I was always on my guard, because there were some stray dogs around the area who could be very aggressive.

I'd instantly start commanding George non-stop, and I could see that people walking past thought I was going over the top, because I would literally be giving a running commentary, the whole time the strays was near.

'Stay, George. Good boy, stay close, stay there . . .' I'd tell him, over and over again. I made no apologies to the people who gave me weird looks, and I still command George like this now. It's what dogs like him need, especially when they are off the lead.

Not all dog owners share my views on discipline, of course, and one day a bloke with a pit bull terrier came down the High Street and stood talking to his mate for a few minutes, right in front of me and George. He wasn't watching his dog at all, and the next thing I knew the bloody animal had George round the throat.

'I'm really sorry, mate!' he said when we'd prised them apart. 'I can't apologise enough.'

'Don't apologise,' I said. 'Get him fucking trained. That could have been a kid he went for.'

I'm not saying George is perfect – far from it. He is a dog at the end of the day, and he has some bad habits I can't seem to break. One of his worst is eating any old rubbish he finds on the street. It doesn't matter how much dog food he's eaten, if he sniffs out a discarded take-away box full of old chicken bones and chips, he'll scoff the lot, cardboard and all.

'Oi, you dirty bugger,' I always tell him. I get him wormed regularly, so I know that's not the problem. He's just a greedy git – it's in his nature.

His worst characteristic by a mile is losing concentration when we're crossing the road. He still needs watching like a hawk, because Shoreditch is very busy, and if I'm not constantly badgering him to stay close and walk by my side he could easily make a mistake.

I had a sharp reminder of this about a year after we moved into the area. It was a Friday night and I was crossing the road by the petrol station when a bus turned the corner and stopped in the middle of the road. I walked in front of it, but when I stopped to check for oncoming traffic George just carried on, clearing the bus and walking into the path of a car. He was hit at about 20mph and literally went under the front of the car.

'George!' I screamed. Our eyes actually met as he went down. It was bloody terrifying, but George immediately stood up and let me lead him to the side of the road. I waved the car driver on, indicating it was not his fault, and sat George on my lap on the side of the road.

'Is he alright, mate?' a bloke at the bus stop asked. 'That turned my stomach.'

'Looks like it,' I said. 'You alright, George?'

He looked at me and blinked, like he was saying: 'What was all that about?'

I sat there on the pavement with him and checked his ribcage and every inch of his body for broken bones. There wasn't a scratch on him and he wasn't even shaking. I think I'd had a bigger shock than him, and when I play that back in my mind it still makes me shudder. I started keeping him on the lead for a while after that.

After a few months of sitting on the pavement and drawing, George and I became part of the furniture of the street, and I felt like we finally belonged somewhere. I hadn't had that feeling since I was a small kid in President House.

'Oh look, there's that guy,' I'd hear people say. 'He sits there every day, drawing. The dog never moves. Look at him!'

My sketches of the buildings were getting better all the time, and I'd find myself getting completely engrossed in what I was doing. People would stand over me and watch me draw, but sometimes I barely noticed them because I was so lost in my work. Hours would pass as I focussed on smaller and smaller details and all the while George would sit quietly by my side taking in the streetlife and barely moving a muscle. Eventually, people started asking how much I sold the pictures for, and before long I was charging £10 or £20 a drawing. They weren't even properly finished; I'd done them purely for practice and would have added more detail had I known people were going to buy them, but they were snapped up anyway.

'What else do you draw?' a lady asked me one day.

'What do you want me to draw?' I replied.

'Can you do your dog for me?'

I looked at George, sitting there all handsome and proud-looking in his coat with the cup in front of him, and I wasn't at all surprised she wanted a drawing of him. Plenty of people had taken his photo like that, and I'd been planning to have a go at drawing him anyhow, and looking at him just then something clicked. He looked so peaceful and calm; I wanted to capture it all.

'Course I can,' I said. 'Can you come back in half an hour and I'll have it ready for you?'

'That's fine, thanks. How much do you charge?'

'£10 to you, madam.'

I tried to look and sound as confident as possible, but to tell the truth I wasn't really sure how it would turn out. I'd never drawn a dog before in my life, but then this was George . . .

As soon as I started drawing I could sense that this was a big step for me. Portraiture isn't just about getting the image down on the page, it's about capturing the spirit of the person or animal you're drawing. I knew George inside out by this time – all his little quirks and moods, his mannerisms – and I wanted to do him justice. It was a totally different skill to drawing the buildings around me, but as soon as I started it, I knew it would be special. I got his bright eyes, the turn of his little stomach, his stubby nose. But more than that, I got *him* – my best friend. It was as good as I could have hoped for. When I put down my pens and looked at the drawing, I realised something else: it was the first piece of art I'd ever fully completed, and, what's more, it was my first commission. George was the reason I'd picked up my pens, and now George was the reason I could call myself an artist. Underneath the drawing, I simply wrote 'George the Dog. Shoreditch, London.'

George the Dog.

Shoreditch. London :

'I love it!' the lady shrieked when she came back later. Though I say so myself, I wasn't surprised by her reaction. I knew I'd really captured George, but seeing the lady's reaction confirmed it.

'I'm really pleased,' I said, calmly. 'I can't tell you how pleased I am. Have a nice day!'

I kept my cool but inside I was screaming: 'Fuck me! I've sold my first commission! I'm a frigging artist!'

After that I started drawing George regularly, and I began to sell drawings every day. Workers from the shops and offices and local business people were starting to talk about us, and there was suddenly a buzz around Shoreditch about me and George and my artwork.

I could feel myself edging forward. I was still living below the breadline, but the plans I had to go up to Hampstead and draw the houses were put on the back burner, because I could feel I was onto something better here. Given time, I was going to really make this pay, I was sure.

'I'm gonna do it,' I'd tell George when I felt we both needed convincing. 'I'm gonna make it.'

He always looked at me like I was losing my marbles when I said that, but I knew I was going to prove myself to him one day.

'Don't look like that, miserable bastard,' I'd say. 'Just you wait and see.'

Chapter Seventeen

I was sitting drawing in my usual spot one Friday afternoon when two guys came over and asked if they could commission me to do a piece for a book they were putting together. This was new. I knew the word was getting out about my drawings, but a book was something else. That sounded professional.

'Sound good,' I said, eyes lighting up. 'What's the book?'

The guys introduced themselves as Steven Moffett and Steven Dray and explained that the publication was called *Shoreditch Unbound*. They were both creative types, and they started explaining that it would be a limited-edition collection of articles, images and art chronicling the history of Shoreditch and showcasing the talent in the area today. I found out later that it would include work by artists ranging from Tracey Emin to Gilbert & George.

I was beginning to get to know the street art scene pretty well. I'd seen groups of people going on tours, looking at weird and wonderful things like painted-on used chewing gum that was stuck to the pavement, the work of an artist called Ben Wilson. I'd wandered round the corner to Great Eastern Street to have a look at the Village Underground wall which was used for public art and has artists from all over the world come and paint on it. And more and more, in conversation with locals, I'd hear mention of names of famous street artists like Stik and Thierry Noir as if I ought to know them, but to tell the truth they didn't mean a thing to me. I confessed my ignorance to a homeless friend and he put me right.

'Have a look down Rivington Street,' he told me. 'Stik does the stick men and Thierry Noir is that French bloke who painted the Berlin Wall. He does those brightly coloured faces with the white eyes and fat lips.' I went and checked them out and was totally mesmerised by their work.

Knowing all this, I was amazed to have been approached for a book that would feature some of these artists, not to mention the likes of Tracey Emin and Gilbert & George. I'd actually met Gilbert & George on the High Street a few times. They lived just down the road on Brick Lane and I'd often see them walking around together. We were on nodding terms, and had been for a while. They would walk past by my pitch at the same time each evening, always dressed in their matching tweed suits. Every time they passed by they would have a look at what I was drawing and give me a few pointers. I was unbelievably proud that I'd managed to attract the attention of two artists of their calibre.

I'd never heard of ROA, I have to confess, but I found out later he was a world-renowned Belgian street artist, known for drawing giant black-and-white birds and animals. He had first made his mark in London after painting a massive rabbit on the wall of a recording studio in Hackney, and he had some amazing pieces around Shoreditch too.

I met Steven and Steven again two days later, up at Columbia Road flower market on the Sunday, where I handed them a couple of pictures. On one sheet I'd drawn studies of three men's faces, and on the other I'd done the Leather & Suede shop and the crumbling building above and beside it. I signed my work 'John Dolan, Shoreditch High Street 2011', charged the guys £150, and signed something that gave them copyright.

I thought no more about it. I had no idea whether the book would be successful or even if I'd make it into print, but whatever happened it was flattering to have been asked to contribute. It made me feel even more a part of the community, and was another boost for my self-confidence.

Not long after that, George and I were coming out of my flat one day when I suddenly felt a crippling pain in both my legs and literally couldn't move. An older guy was coming out of his flat opposite at the same time, and I noticed he was on crutches. 'Have you got a spare pair of crutches?' I called out, because I'd left mine in the flat.

'No, fuck off. There's an ambulance there – ask them.'

There was an ambulance down the street but I wasn't capable of moving, and so I phoned for an ambulance of my own and was taken to the hospital for an X-ray. George came in the back with me, and I held on to him as hard as I could. I was thinking how difficult it would be to look after him with a broken ankle. Thankfully, the doctors told me that nothing was messed up too badly and it was just my arthritis flaring up really badly; later that day I managed to hobble home on a new pair of crutches, dosed up on painkillers.

A month or so after that I was on a bus with George when I saw the old guy who'd told me to fuck off. 'My name's Les,' he said, coming over to introduce himself. 'I'm sorry about the crutches and all that. I was in agony myself that day. I do apologise.'

It turned out that Les was a gay man who was HIV-positive and suffering from osteoporosis. We chatted for a while and hit it off, and afterwards he invited me to his flat for a coffee. I found myself telling him a bit about my life, and what I was doing on the High Street.

'My art is all I've got,' I said. 'It's my only hope of turning my life around.'

I hadn't confided in anybody else, except George, and it was really good to have somebody to chat to. I could see that Les appreciated my company too. 'Come round again,' he said. 'I want to see your work in the book, when it comes out.'

I think he was quite lonely, and I promised I'd call in again soon. In time, Les became a very good friend. I'd pop in to see how he was every couple of days, and if my hot water packed up he'd let me use his washing machine, and I'd slip him twenty quid to say thanks. I'd rib him by calling him an 'old queen' and 'Mum', but he really did become a bit like a mum to me. I could talk to him about anything, and he fussed over me and George something rotten.

I told Les all about everything that was happening on the street, and he would tell me what was going on in the rest of the world, because he was always watching the news on TV. I'd given up watching it, because I was fed up to the back teeth of hearing about all the benefits cuts, but

Les was all over it and every time I saw him he would tell me what David Cameron was up to next.

The conversation was always interesting, and I'd look at George and say: 'See, at least I get some sense and decent chat out of Les. Not like you!' It made Les laugh when I ribbed George like that, and so I did it all the time.

'Oi, George, you're the only one not on crutches. Can't you put the kettle on for a change?' I'd say, and Les would piss himself laughing.

One day a woman came up to me on the High Street and told me she had a gallery somewhere in Brixton. I was drawing a lot of faces at the time; she seemed particularly interested in those and gave me her card.

I hadn't even decided what to do about her before a couple of other women approached me. They were talking about putting on an exhibition, and they said they had a gallery too. I arranged to meet them the next day, but it was pissing down with rain and I put it off.

A similar thing happened another month or so later, when a group of arty types came over and told me they were making a video in the area with the R&B singer Lemar. They asked if I was interested in talking to them about my work and we arranged a time to meet, but either they were late or they never showed up, and I eventually gave up and went home.

I told Les about all of these things, and it was good to have a second opinion. 'Should I have been a bit more patient, or proactive? What do you think?'

'Listen to your gut,' Les always said. 'Did any of them feel right?'

'No, or I would have followed them up.'

'Exactly. You'll know when it's right. Take all the approaches as compliments and bide your time. It'll happen soon enough.'

I listened to Les and just carried on doing what I was doing, sitting with George on the High Street every day, in all weathers. By now I was charging £20 for some of my pictures of George, because I spent longer on them and added more detail, especially when I drew him in his sheepskin coat.

People started asking me to draw pictures of their partners or their dogs, and I'd do sketches for them while they waited, as well as continuing to draw the buildings on the High Street. There was a lot of development and construction work going on and, though I hadn't exactly planned it this way, my pictures were chronicling some of the changes along the High Street.

There was an old billboard next to 187 Shoreditch High Street, and just to spice things up a bit, I started to write my own slogans on it when I included it in my drawings.

'David Cameron is a CNUT' was my favourite because, thanks to Les, I was well up to speed on the mess the government was continuing to make of the benefits system.

The changes Cameron brought in were meant to weed out anyone who was exploiting the system, but those people made up the tiniest fraction of claimants. The vast majority were people like me, needing extra support while they were trying to get themselves out of the shit. If I hadn't had George with me, I know I would have gone out thieving all over again, because it was the only way, with no job history and a criminal record, that I could have brought in enough money to keep myself above water.

Anyhow, as luck would have it, these billboard drawings went down a treat. Even young girls would come up, coo over George and then say: 'Have you got any of the c**t drawings? Can you do me one please?' It was a bit jarring to hear them speak that kind of language, but I wasn't complaining. A sale was a sale.

The vibe on the street was great with all this going on, and I like to think that George's sarcastic looks were diminishing as he lapped up the fuss and attention he was receiving.

'Got to hand it to you, we're doing alright,' I reckon he was thinking.

Chapter Eighteen

One evening in August 2012, a young, posh-looking bloke walked up to me and introduced himself as Richard Howard-Griffin. He explained that he worked with and represented several well-known street artists. He had his mate Cityzen Kane with him, who is renowned for his 3D sculptures of spirit masks that decorate walls around the East End.

Richard – or Griff, as he went by – was very enthusiastic about what he did, and he told me he was interested in working with me.

'I really like your work,' he said in his plummy accent. 'It would be great if we could work on something together.' He seemed thoughtful and was clearly a smart bloke. He only looked to be in his early twenties, but he told me he had an office and a studio on Rivington Street, just round the corner from where I was sitting.

I mentioned *Shoreditch Unbound* and the fact I'd been approached by a few other people, and told him I would certainly be interested in hearing what he had to offer.

Cityzen Kane bought one of my 'David Cameron is a CNUT' drawings, and Griff asked me if I could draw a bigger picture of 187 Shoreditch High Street but with a blank billboard, which of course I said I could. He went to the art shop up the road and got me a big canvas and a load of pens, including a Magic Marker, and I promised I'd get the picture to him as soon as I could.

No other promises were made, no meetings arranged and no deals struck, but I had a good feeling about Griff. He had energy and vision and he hadn't talked any bollocks. I liked that. We were going to work well together; I could feel it in my bones.

It took me a few days to draw the large building picture, and I did it using the Magic Marker, which gave it a kind of pop-art feel. As I was drawing, sitting on the High Street, somebody approached me and asked if they could buy it.

'Sorry, no, it's for an art dealer,' I said, which gave me a bit of a buzz, and I'm sure made George smirk.

I left the billboard blank, exactly as Griff had asked me to, and I was very pleased with the finished result. Even George raised his eyebrows when he saw it.

'Not bad at all,' I said. 'Even if I do say so myself.'

George just turned away and sat quietly in front of his cup. I think the jury was still out in his mind, because he's a sceptical bugger like that.

A few days later I took the giant canvas to Griff's studio wrapped in a bin liner. It knocked him sideways. He held it up and looked at it from every angle, holding it against different walls and propping it up with one outstretched arm and standing back to admire it.

Griff checking out the big canvas.

'I like it,' he said. 'I really do.' And this was when he told me about his idea. He wanted to invite street artists to put their own work in the advertising billboard within my picture that I'd left blank. To be honest I didn't really get the concept. To my mind I could add my own work on the billboard, as I had done with the slogans. What I didn't know then was that Griff wasn't just thinking of asking any old street artists to contribute – he was going to ask the best in the world.

I left the canvas with him, and he promised to get back to me, which I knew he would.

In the meantime, I had Griff's card in my pocket, and I started to ask one or two people what he was like. One of the local business people who knew of him said, 'Oh him – you can't trust him,' and I burst out laughing.

'He's definitely the one for me,' I told Les afterwards. 'Posh boy or not, we might have a few things in common!'

That September, Steven and Steven turned up again, bringing with them a newly printed copy of *Shoreditch Unbound*. My drawings of the three male faces and the Leather & Suede shop featured across two A4-sized pages, just before a big glossy image of Boy George. I was bowled over, and I scanned the pages excitedly, looking at images and articles on greats like Tracey Emin and Gilbert & George and the street artists Stik and Thierry Noir.

The book was really unusual, presented in a ring-binder style, and was retailing for £80. It was very stylish, and when I saw my work published for posterity, it gave me a big old lump in my throat.

'You know what, that's my proudest achievement,' I told the guys. 'I can't tell you what that means to me.'

'See that, George,' I said later, as we were flicking through the book in my bedsit. 'I'm a published artist!'

He had nothing to say to that – no wry looks or anything. I'd like to think he could feel things happening, and he was just waiting to see what the next step would be, just like I was.

The whole *Shoreditch Unbound* experience filled me with confidence, and one day I decided to take the book into a local gallery, to see if I could drum up interest in my art and maybe talk my way into an exhibition. I was brimming with pride and enthusiasm as I showed off my published work, but the gallery owner had no interest in it whatsoever, and didn't even have the courtesy to let me down gently. I was practically sent away with a flea in my ear, and that knocked the stuffing out of me. I realised then that it was going to take a lot more than having a couple of sketches printed in a book to break into the established art world.

I carried on drawing George the Dogs and the High Street and billboard pictures and selling them for £10 and £20 each, biding my time. The gallery owner's reaction had been a setback, but once I'd got over the initial disappointment it didn't stop me believing in myself. Thanks to *Shoreditch Unbound*, I felt sure it was only a matter of time before I made it as an artist, I just had to keep working hard whilst waiting for my opportunity. I was very optimistic that the right one would come up eventually and, even though I hadn't seen him for a while, I still had a very good feeling that Griff was going to be the one to move things on for me.

As time went on I occasionally added colour to my drawings, and I came up with a couple of other slogans for the billboard that people liked. 'Bollox.com' was one, poking fun at all the random rubbish on the internet, and 'Sex, drugs and rock and roll, and a nice cup of tea' was another, because it reflected the fact that I was getting on a bit!

In February 2013, Griff came over to see me on the High Street. It was pissing down yet again and George and I were under an umbrella. I remember hoping that I wouldn't have to spend another winter on the street after this one. I hadn't badgered Griff at all, even though about six months had gone by since our first meeting. I wasn't worried; I knew that he would show up when the time was right.

Griff explained that the only reason he hadn't been in touch was because he'd been incredibly busy, organising a couple of big street-art festivals that were coming up in May and June in Dulwich and Chichester.

We talked about the billboard idea again and the plan to collaborate with street artists from all over the world.

He explained a little more and I listened with interest, not sure what I was letting myself in for. My notoriety was growing, but I'd only just started to see myself as a proper artist, and the idea of collaborating with other artists at this stage felt like a big leap into the unknown.

Griff was insistent though and told me that in a couple of days he'd be meeting Stik and Thierry Noir in the cafe on the corner, just over the road from where I was sitting.

'I want you to come and meet them,' he said. I knew the two names well by then and had seen a couple of their murals but I still didn't consider myself very familiar with their work, so I asked Griff to tell me more.

He explained that Stik had been painting his stick men around the East End for more than a decade and was now receiving worldwide recognition. He was also producing a lot of successful shows and working to support charities like Amnesty International, which impressed me. And Thierry Noir had become world famous for illegally painting miles of the Berlin Wall and had worked with the likes of U2 at the height of his notoriety. Griff had met Noir in Berlin at around the same time he met me, and had invited him over to Shoreditch to paint the Village Underground wall on Holywell Lane, along with Stik. The Village Underground (or VU) wall is the most prestigious street art wall in London. They were going to meet up together in a local cafe to start sketching out their plans.

I agreed to meet up with them too, but I was still a little unsure about how the whole thing would work. When I'd said goodbye to Griff, I looked over to George to see what he was thinking. He had a look that could only mean one thing: 'Good luck mate. You're gonna need it'.

Two days later, when we arrived at the cafe, Griff was already there with two blokes in high-vis jackets who looked like a couple of road sweepers, plus a young girl he introduced as his assistant, Carina.

I was wondering when the famous artists would turn up, when Griff introduced me to the two unassuming-looking blokes sat with him in high-vis jackets.

'This is Stik,' Griff said, smiling at the younger of the two men. 'And this is Thierry Noir,' he added, nodding politely and eagerly towards the older gentleman.

Griff clearly had a lot of respect for these two artists: the smile on his face proved it. He was treating them like a couple of rock stars, and quite rightly so, because in the street-art world these two men are legends. I found myself behaving in the same way as Griff. It was like we were in the presence of greatness; I was caught up in the energy surrounding the meeting and felt honoured to be there. It was humbling to think that Thierry Noir was painting the Berlin Wall while I was an eighteen-year-old thief, about to serve my first sentence at Feltham. Now here we were, sitting together in a cafe in Shoreditch, drinking tea and about to discuss the possibility of collaborating together on a work of art. It didn't seem real.

I understood Griff's big idea now, and I have to hand it to posh boy, it was a bloody good one. Starting with Stik and Thierry Noir, he was going to ask high-profile street artists to put their work inside the blank billboards of my Shoreditch High Street drawings, just as if it were something they were painting on the street. As well as introducing us to each other, Griff wanted to find out what Stik and Noir thought about the idea.

'I like it; it's a very cool idea,' Stik said as Griff showed him my work. Thierry agreed. 'It's a really clever concept,' he said. 'And I like your work, John. You could really be onto something.'

They were both friendly and encouraging, and coming from them it meant an awful lot. I could feel the adrenalin running through me. Here were two well-known and respected artists and not only were giving me the time of day, they were up for the idea of working together. What's more, they made it clear they were both prepared to work for nothing, to help get the project off the ground, because they knew exactly what it was like to be on the street and starting out like me.

I found out later that Griff had told them I was what he called 'the real deal.' In other words, with my long history of homelessness, I had genuinely come from the street. I was still working on the street, drawing for my survival, and they respected me for that.

I handed Thierry a George the Dog drawing and Stik a few other sketches I had on me, as I wanted to give them something back. They thanked me and wished me luck.

Stik and Thierry Noir hatching plans.

I went along to Griff's office in Rivington Street afterwards, to talk business. George came along too.

'What exactly can you do for me?' I asked Griff when we sat down around his desk.

'John, what do you want me to do for you?' said Griff.

'Make me a rich artist!' I said, half-joking.

'I can do that!' he replied.

'And why would you want to do that for me?'

'Because I'm a nice guy.'

He was clearly being ironic, but George and I still exchanged glances.

'Bollocks!' the shared thought-bubble above our heads said.

I asked Griff straight what he wanted in return, if I effectively took him on as my art dealer. He told me we'd start by splitting the profits on anything we sold.

'Fifty-fifty?' I said, laughing. 'Blimey, you don't want much do you?!'

We were both smiling at the end of this conversation, and we shook hands on the deal. I wasn't going to start arguing about money, but neither was I going to sign anything. Griff was fine with that. I didn't tell him this, but all I really wanted was to not spend another winter on the street and I hoped he would be able to help.

Griff loaded me up with plenty of good-quality paper and pens and I went back to the pavement and carried on producing billboard drawings. It wasn't long before Griff was back with more news and ideas. After the positive response he'd got from Stik and Noir, he was hopeful that he could get artists from all around the world to collaborate on the large billboard drawing – and we're not talking just any artists. Griff wanted to send out screenprinted copies to all the famous street artists he know around the world, from Russia to Berlin and Colombia to LA.

This sounded bloody ambitious to me. I had no idea how good Griff's contacts were, so I couldn't judge how realistic this was, but I trusted him after the meeting with Stik and Noir. Don't ask me how or why, but I had a very strong feeling this was all going to work.

Griff said he also wanted me to draw some other, larger-scale buildings around Shoreditch than the ones I was used to doing, and to produce a load more High Street scenes and pictures of George.

'Why?' I asked him. I couldn't see the point of the other drawings he was asking for. They didn't seem to fit with the collaboration idea.

'Because if you can get all that together, we can put on an exhibition,' Griff said. That stopped me in my tracks. My work would be displayed in a gallery? Not only that, it would be a solo show and, if everything went to plan, my work would be endorsed and embellished by the global legends of street art. It was almost too much to bear.

'Exactly how many pictures would you need for that?' I asked. As excited as I was, I needed to be sure I could actually do what he was asking.

'As well as the collaborations with the street artists? Fifty High Streets and fifty George the Dogs,' he said.

This was a shitload of work, especially as I wasn't used to being put under any kind of pressure to draw.

'When would you put the show on?' I asked tentatively.

'In about four or five months.'

'Where?'

'I haven't worked that one out yet.'

'OK, I'd better get back to work pretty bloody quick then,' I said.

I was grinning widely, though my mind was whirring. I wasn't used to having anything like that amount of responsibility on my shoulders, but I certainly didn't want to say or do anything that would screw up this opportunity. It was the biggest chance of my life, and my biggest hope of finally doing something to secure the future for myself and George. It was also my chance to make my family proud.

Chapter Nineteen

'John, I need to know. Have you got a problem?' it was Griff and it was the first time I'd ever seen him pissed off.

I knew immediately what he meant, and I got to my feet sheepishly from the street. I knew this was no time for bullshit.

'What do you mean?'

'Drink, drugs?'

There was no point in trying to deceive him. He'd done an awful lot for me, and I didn't want to break the trust that had developed between us.

'Yes, I have. I've got a drug problem and I have done for many years. I can explain.'

I'm ashamed to say that I had never quite managed to kick my drug habit, even after taking on George. I'd got myself down to the tiniest amount of heroin I could get away with on a daily basis, just enough to stop the with-drawal symptoms from creeping in. People who saw me on the High Street would never have known I had a problem. It had taken Griff a long time to find out. The thing was, I functioned normally and I wasn't the archetypal druggie, looking unkempt and jittery with bad skin and dark circles round my eyes. I'd smartened myself up since I had my flat and I managed to work and talk extremely well with people on the street every single day. Unfortunately I just hadn't been able to kick the last remnants of my habit, however many times I tried.

I told Griff everything; I owed him the truth. I also wanted him to know that I hadn't tried to pull the wool over his eyes. I was so used to controlling my problem the way I did that it was second nature to me, and I never felt the need to discuss it with anybody.

He listened, then said calmly: 'John, I need to know you can produce the show. Can I rely on you to come up with the goods?'

'Yes, I can do it, and I won't let you down,' I said. 'I'll go to the doctor tomorrow and get myself on a withdrawal programme. I've never had an incentive like this before. I'll do it.'

Not long after that, Griff made what he calls his 'crossing the Rubicon' decision, and it was one that had much more to do with intuition and gut feeling than business. He offered me a £1,000 advance on all the High Street and George the Dog pictures, hoping that would help keep me focussed and give me the boost I needed to carry out my part of the bargain.

'I'll take £100,' I told him, because I didn't want to fritter the money away, and I didn't have a bank account. 'Can you keep hold of the other £900 for me?'

I think Griff was surprised by my reaction, but he agreed, and he kept the money locked away in his office for me, telling me it was there whenever I wanted it.

Griff has told me since that he had never experienced anything like the pressure he felt in the subsequent few months leading up to the exhibition. 'Not all art shows have a person's life riding on it,' he tells people now, but that was the case with me. It was make or break for my finances, my health, my whole life. And George's future depended on it too.

Griff makes light of it now, but at the time it was no laughing matter. He had only been in the art business for a couple of years when we started planning the show, and he was already spending money hand over fist organising street art festivals in Dulwich and Chichester. He'd shelled out hundreds of pounds in materials for me and roped in two top street artists in Stik and Thierry Noir to get the ball rolling. Now he'd given me an advance before the drawing for the collab, as he called it, had even been produced, and he was regularly working until 2 a.m. to pull everything together. It really, really had to work.

Even with all this pressure, Griff had a brainwave about the drawing for the collab. If he could get me access to a nearby rooftop I would be able to include the Village Underground wall in my drawing, and that would be a better place for the street art to appear than on the billboard. The London skyline would be amazing from high above Shoreditch High Street too and it would be a new challenge for me to draw it all. He'd worked hard to get me access to the top of an office block behind Tesco, which was opposite my regular pitch and towered above the High Street. Griff would now literally come and pick me off the pavement and frogmarch me up there, easel, George and all. Whenever he wasn't around he got his assistant Carina to chaperone me, as he'd said he would. The location was superb. As well as the Village Underground wall I could see the converted train carriages that were used as art studios behind it, and beyond those were the Heron Tower and Broadgate Tower skyscrapers, with the tip of the Gherkin visible to their left. In the foreground I had the overground railway line curving in from the left, with the busy road below and the infamous Chariots sauna tucked behind the tracks.

As soon as I started work on the skyline I felt a surge of confidence, and I started to believe in myself more than ever. I wanted the drawing to be absolutely perfect and was taking my time, working hard every day. It was a long-winded process, and the conditions weren't great. The office workers got a bit sniffy when they saw me with George, carrying my easel and all my clutter, making my way past their places of business. The weather wasn't brilliant either, and I lost several days because it was too wet and windy to be perched up on the rooftop. As time ticked by, I ended up having photographs taken of the skyline, so I could work on the picture in my flat in the evening.

To help publicise my work Griff got a local filmmaker, Will Robson-Scott, to make a short documentary about me. I thoroughly enjoyed the experience because Will took me back to all my old haunts, Pentonville Prison included. Along the way I'd be telling taxi drivers: 'We're making this film because I'm just about to explode on the art scene!'

While Griff was away at the street-art festival in Chichester, I was approached by a couple of rock musicians who turned out to be in the band Heaven's Basement. They were due to be interviewed on a Radio 1 show with DJ Alice Levine. The format of the show was that guests had to take in a present for Alice and her male co-host.

The two musicians asked me to draw a picture of the DJs, which I did. At the time, women's faces were not my strong point at all, and I asked the guys to explain this to Alice, as I wasn't happy with how her picture turned out – in fact, I made a right balls-up of it. As soon as the musicians started to pass on my message on air, Alice said: 'Don't tell me, his strong point is not drawing women's faces!' This got a big laugh, but the upshot was that I was being talked about. The musicians made sure to describe me in detail, telling Alice all about how I sat drawing on the pavement, with George beside me.

I took this as yet more proof that I was really making a name for myself as an artist. I was being talked about on national radio. Everything was coming together as I'd hoped it might.

I've never worked so hard in all my life as I did in the spring of 2013. I was knocking out High Street drawings and George the Dogs as fast as I could and selling them to passers-by to keep me and George fed and housed, and then Carina would appear and marshal me up to the rooftop to work on the drawing for the show. I was going cross-eyed and my fingers were aching by the time it went dark, but the work and my sense of purpose made me feel bloody fantastic.

I have to admit that when I was a teenager, bumming around with no job and no prospects, I didn't see the point in slaving away, only to give a load of your hard-earned cash away to the taxman. Now I had a totally different view. At long last, I was learning how fulfilling it was to do an honest, productive day's work.

Les would invite me round for dinner sometimes, and I'd bend his ear about how hard I was working.

'I'm not giving you any sympathy,' he'd say. 'Keep going. You're doing all the right things.' George would sit beside him nodding in agreement, and after we'd eaten I'd pick up my pen and draw a couple more George the Dog pictures while we carried on chatting and George kipped on the floor.

Griff was desperate to get the skyline picture copied and sent out to the street artists, and he was checking up on me every day to see how I was getting on. 'I'm taking my time,' I'd say to him. 'Stop worrying. I'm doing it.'

Griff *was* worrying though, so much so that he decided to put the exhibition back until September. This would not only give me more time to finish the High Streets and George the Dogs he wanted for the show, but it would also give Griff more time to get as many collabs done as possible.

The art business was a whole new world to me, and I was all ears when Griff told me exactly how he planned to get the artists on board. He explained that some artists he knew would be very willing to help and had already shown interest, like Stik and Thierry, but others would need a bit more persuasion, either because they didn't like being asked to do collaborations or because they were just extremely busy and hard to track down. Griff knew a lot of the big names and would see plenty of famous street artists during the festivals he was organising in May and June, but he wanted to get the ball rolling earlier than that if possible.

'ROA's in town,' he said. 'I got him a big wall just off Bethnal Green Road, behind KFC. I want you to go and meet him, take him a billboard picture, explain the concept and ask him if he'll collaborate on it.'

Griff had told me all about ROA and I was horrified at the prospect of having to approach someone of his stature.

'ROA? The guy who does the big monochrome animals and birds? Did the giant hedgehog down Chance Street?'

'Yes, John.'

'But he's a legend.'

'Yes. He's also a "zero compromise" artist.'

'What do you mean?'

'He won't do anything he doesn't want to do.'

I was very daunted, but Griff explained that I'd have a far better chance of getting ROA to collaborate if I went to meet him in person and tell him what I was doing. He wanted me to drop the drawing off so he could make up his own mind about whether to do it or not.

It seemed too cheeky to me, but Griff was very persuasive.

'Meet me up there on Tuesday and I'll introduce you,' he said.

I reluctantly agreed. Griff had lined up a reporter from the *Metro* to interview ROA, and he said he'd already told the guy: 'You can meet two ends of the spectrum. ROA the superstar artist, and John Dolan the artist who is still on the street.'

I didn't want to let Griff down, but I was as nervous as hell when George and I made our way to Bethnal Green Road. It was pouring with rain and the whole way there I felt like turning on my heel and going back to the High Street or my flat, just to avoid the stress of approaching ROA.

Griff was standing with his assistant Carina and the artist Christiaan Nagel, who is known for his mushroom sculptures, which he's installed in some weird and wonderful places all over the world.

'Right, ROA's having a break and talking to the *Metro* reporter,' Griff said, leading us all down an alleyway. 'John, you need to just get in and talk to him when you see your chance.'

I looked at ROA in awe, and then we all stood around for a few minutes while he finished giving his interview to the *Metro*. The next thing I knew, Griff was doing this crazy thing with his eyebrows, and jerking his head towards ROA, who was eating a sandwich. 'Now's your chance,' Griff said. 'Go and talk to him.'

I took a deep breath and reluctantly edged towards ROA and introduced myself. The *Metro* guy was still there, and he realised this was the 'two ends of the spectrum' meeting that Griff had talked to him about. The reporter asked me one or two questions, which helped break the ice, and then George got in on the act too by gazing longingly at ROA's lunch. We had a photograph taken, which really captures the moment. I had a pen and paper with me and was sketching a building, ROA was eating his sandwich and George was eyeing up the food. It's a superb picture.

Anyway, I was still feeling very nervous about asking ROA to collaborate on my work, and now I could see that he was ready to get back to his mural.

'Are you here tomorrow?' I asked, deciding to quit while I was ahead for the time being.

'Yes,' he said.

'OK if I come back tomorrow?'

'Yes, no problem,' he said.

The next day I found ROA on his own, listening to music, perched high up on a cherry picker. I stood and watched in fascination how he controlled his spray can, and I bided my time before going and talking to him again.

Eventually he came off the cherry picker and went up some steps to a nearby rooftop, so he could take a look at how his work was progressing. If Griff had been there, I knew this was the moment he'd have been saying 'Go on, just do it. Go and talk to him,' so I did.

ROA was listening to grime music on his phone. I'm a big fan of grime too so we got talking about it and we really hit it off. I ended up just chilling out with him and chatting for two hours, knowing all the time I'd have to pluck up courage and talk to him about my work before I left.

Eventually I just came out with it, explaining Griff's idea to ask street artists to draw on the billboard, and telling him how the idea had progressed and that I was working on a skyline picture too, so artists could draw on the Village Underground wall.

'Don't suppose you would consider doing one?' I asked.

'Fine,' he said, just like that. 'No problem.'

All that stress I'd had about asking him had turned out to be for nothing. He was a lovely guy, definitely not someone I should have been afraid of talking to. I thanked him and stayed and chatted for a bit longer. On my way off the rooftop I put the billboard drawing in his bag and crossed my fingers.

ROA's mural was an amazing melee of intertwined birds and animals, and caused a big sensation. The following week the *Metro* feature appeared, and to my amazement I was included in the article. I hadn't expected to make it into print at all, and I was completely blown away, not least because the article also mentioned Banksy. 'Fucking hell,' I thought, looking at George in disbelief. 'I'm mentioned in the same article as ROA and Banksy, in a London newspaper!'

I thought Griff could do anything at this point. I totally believed in him and really admired his zest and determination. I thought that if he could get me in the *Metro* like this, absolutely anything was possible. He was still looking for suitable premises for the show and the date was yet to be fixed, but it was definitely happening, and seeing my name in print was further proof something big was happening. I was convinced I wasn't just going to put on any old exhibition, I was going to become a Johnny Big Cheese and use my art to inspire other homeless people.

'Can you get Bruce Springsteen to come to the show?' I asked, and I was only half joking, because in my eyes Griff had the best contacts book in London and could pull any strings he liked.

Griff laughed his head off, and I can see how funny that is, because I now know he's just an ordinary twat.

I phoned my sister Jackie on the day the *Metro* article was published. Throughout my time in Shoreditch I'd been keeping my sister Jackie informed about what was happening in my life, phoning her every six months or so as I always had done over the years we'd been apart. I'd explained about me sitting on the pavement with George, and I'd told Jackie all about the dog having the cup in front of him. When I first started to draw I told her about that too, because news travels fast in the East End and I didn't want her finding out from anybody else what I was up to.

'Read the *Metro*,' I told her. 'I'm mentioned in the same article as Banksy!'

'Really?' she said. 'Are you serious?'

Now I had something to ask her and this seemed like the perfect time.

'Jackie, I want you to come to the opening night of the exhibition. There's a big buzz about me around Shoreditch at the moment. You have to be there!'

Jackie listened as I explained how I felt about the show, and how important it was for her to be there.

'I've stayed away from you for all these years because of my lifestyle,' I said. 'But I'm finally ready to have my family around me again. It'll be my way of saying sorry, and making you proud of your little brother, at long last.'

'Yes, John, it's about time!' Jackie joked. I'm not sure she knew what else to say – it was a big ask after not seeing each other for so many years. This was the very first time in my life I'd phoned her with good news, and it must have sounded very unlikely that old Burglar Bill here had suddenly turned into a bona fide artist, and one who was going to have a solo exhibition in London.

I asked after David and Malcolm and told Jackie I wanted them to come to the show too. 'Please persuade them all to come, Jack? It will mean the world to me to have you all there.'

Poor Jackie was really put on the spot. 'I can't promise,' she said. 'I know David and Malcolm are both working and are both really busy . . .'

It was obvious she wasn't quite sure whether to believe this show was really happening, and she clearly couldn't speak for David and Malcolm anyway.

'Keep me posted,' Jackie said before we said goodbye. 'Let me know when you've got the date set and all that. Good luck, John.'

'I will,' I told her. 'And I can't wait.'

Chapter Twenty

I wanted and needed our show to be a success and the fact that I'd gone to meet ROA in the pouring rain when I really didn't feel like it showed Griff how serious I was. It gave him faith in everything we were doing. I could feel the momentum building all the time, and I'd often wake up in the morning already thinking about the show, feeling full of excitement and anticipation.

The skyline picture had taken me seven hard weeks to complete, but it was finally done. It was without doubt the best drawing I had produced. In May, Griff went to the street art festival he was organising in Dulwich, taking a load of copies of the skyline print with him. I stayed behind on the High Street, drawing all day every day, producing the rest of the work for the show, as well as earning a few quid on the side to keep myself and George afloat.

I'd get so into my work most days that it became almost meditative; George would sit quietly beside me and I'd work silently, not noticing the time passing or even the people on the street, unless they spoke to me directly.

Stik would come over occasionally and sit with us. He's from a homeless background too, and we had a lot in common. We were beginning to forge a true friendship. He offered me lots of encouragement, telling me I had talent and deserved every success, and I was grateful to him for it, because I *did* need reminding of this sometimes.

Despite all the excitement and energy in my life, I still had moments when my depression would slowly rear its ugly head and kick me in the nuts, to remind me that it had never left. That's the trouble with having a history of mental health problems. I didn't just feel blue or down; my depression is a medical condition that I have no control over when it decides to pay me a visit. And when it did I would plunge into extremely pessimistic moods.

'What if all this is just a flash in the pan,' I said to Stik one particularly bad day.

'No it isn't, John. You need to keep believing in yourself.' He was guiding me, spurring me on all the time, and it really helped.

George, as always, continued to be a constant source of inspiration. He was my talisman, and I'd look at him sometimes just to remind myself how far I'd come since we met. I'd been a total mess when I got him, and look where we were now. Somehow deep down, I knew the show was going to be a success, but I told myself that whatever happened next, I'd already achieved so much in my life, thanks to George.

'You bastard,' I'd still tell him, all the time. It didn't matter if he was trying to steal a bit of food or behaving himself impeccably, curled up on the floor beside me while I was drawing.

'You're a bastard, you know that, don't you,' I'd say to him, and he'd look at me with eyes that said 'Takes one to know one.' We were a couple of lost souls who'd found each other and were now tied together for ever, come what may. Whatever happened after the show, I knew I would carry on drawing and earning an honest living at last, and I knew I would never go back to prison, because George was by my side to keep me on the straight and narrow.

The one black cloud hanging over me and threatening to destroy everything was my drug problem. I still hadn't managed to kick my habit. I'd got as far as finding out exactly what help was available and where to get it. I'd made a promise to Griff to sort myself out in time for the show but it wasn't easy to keep. I was still trying to find the courage to go to the doctor's because I knew just how difficult it would be with the stress of the upcoming show and all the work I still had to complete.

I kept telling myself I had to do it before the show, and that became my goal in life. I owed it to Griff, and to everyone else who'd worked with me and believed in me. The success and the positive response Griff got in Dulwich was all the more reason to do it. I had to start believing that if I could come this far, then I could go a little further and get myself clean.

Griff had started to get feedback about the collab, and he and ROA had the idea to give artists the freedom to add their work to other parts of the cityscape, as well as to the Village Underground wall.

'I think we should use real world physics,' he explained to me on the phone one day, 'and suggest that the artists only paint spots that could be achieved in real life. What do you think?'

'I get what you're saying, posh boy,' I said, trying to wind him up. 'You mean just do the sides of walls and train lines, like they would if they were painting on the street?'

'Exactly. It will be like fantasy street art.'

'Sounds good to me. Quite like the concept. Real world physics, eh. What d'you think, George?'

George looked at me blankly. We were in Griff's hands, and that was fine by me for a change. I was happy to leave this part of the job to him. By this point I'd heard enough and seen enough of what he could do to know that I could trust him. Thierry Noir was at the event with Griff in Dulwich and, thanks to the meeting we'd had in the cafe, he already understood the project and was prepared and willing to help. He became the very first artist to add his name and work to my skyline picture. I am so grateful he did because it started a sort of snow-ball effect.

'As well as the VU wall, just do little nooks and cran-nies, the sort of stuff you'd normally do in real life,' Griff mentioned to Thierry, knowing that he was very accommodating and didn't mind being steered in that way.

Thierry was happy to oblige. He did the VU wall with his classic black-outline faces, painted bright red, and he added a couple of little pieces on a poster and the back of the van underneath the railway track.

Along with Thierry, there were a lot of street artists staying with Griff in one house in Dulwich for the festival, including ROA, RUN from Italy, and Liqen from Spain. Griff left Thierry's work out on the table for them all to see and ROA started looking at it one day.

ROA had never actually finished the billboard picture I'd given him on Bethnal Green Road but he obviously remembered meeting me and was still interested in the idea, and what Thierry had done.

Now ROA's input was about to shake things up because all the other artists knew that he only gets involved in interesting projects. One night he sat down at the table and drew a bird on the railway bridge. That one litle sketch really opened the floodgates and after ROA, more artists in the house in Dulwich mucked in: Liqen, for instance, added a big God in the clouds on another print. In the meantime Griff had posted out dozens of prints to other artists from all over the world. Some had already added their work, adhering to the original idea, but after seeing ROA and Liqen's brilliant work, Griff encouraged the other artists to do whatever they wanted.

Stik did a striking collaboration very early on, with a huge yellow stick man that took up the whole of the Broadgate Tower. RUN, Dscreet, BRK and Malarky all did really inventive ones too, adding their interpretation of the concept. Some of the artists even collaborated on the same print, which I hadn't expected at all. The whole thing was just mind-blowing. The distinct style of each artist was bringing to the table meant each collab was poles apart from any of the others. I was humbled and touched by how the artists were reacting to my work. As pieces were completed, Griff started drumming up interest in the show by offering a few of the colabs for sale to his clients, in what he called a 'pre-sale'. This was all new territory to me, and I let Griff get on with it and hoped for the best. I'd included a tiny sketch of George in the skyline picture, which I'd started to do on all my drawings, and I was sure that would be a lucky charm. My faith in the success of the show was growing and I became convinced it was going to be a huge sell-out; I could feel it in my bones.

Collabs began to arrive back in the post, with stamps and postmarks from all around the globe. At least once or twice a week a Fedex guy would turn up at Griff's office with a cardboard postal tube, and then Griff would call me over from the High Street for an 'unveiling'. It was extremely exciting to see each new collab and how the artist had chosen to work with my drawing. George and I would have a photo taken with every new piece, to record the moment.

By now I was getting to know and associate with more and more artists. One day, Rowdy, an old pal of Banksy's, dropped by the studio and did a crocodile on the train track, and then a separate, brightly coloured and incredibly detailed night-time scene. The result was stunning.' I've been saying to Griff I wanted someone to grow a set of balls and just go right over the sky and the whole drawing – and you've done it!' I told him. I was delighted with that. I also loved Cityzen Kane's piece, featuring a giant Hindu god in gold leaf; it's still one of my favourites today.

Some artists asked for a small percentage of the final sale price, but most did it for free because they remembered what it's like to be in my position, coming from nothing and building your reputation from scratch.

Griff did his best to arrange meetings with international artists I hadn't met before whenever they were in town, and it was always a thrill to be introduced to them because with each new connection I felt I was a step closer to becoming one of them – an established artist. But as exhilarating as it all was, in the lead-up to the show I sometimes felt very unsure: as if I had one foot in the past and the other in the future.

Some days I was the old me, still sitting on the street with George and his cup, feeling like a couple of beggars. I was selling a lot of pictures by now because my reputation was growing all the time, but there were still periods when I could go for hours at a time without making a bean, because that's the way it is on the street. During the quiet times I'd suffer from bursts of depression and worry that I was back to square one. It was irrational, because I knew the show was going to be massive, but I couldn't help feeling that way.

Other times I was flying, feeling like a proper artist. People would be crowding round me to watch me draw, or Griff would be on the phone telling me to get myself up to his office, because the Fedex man had brought another tube from Madrid or New York.

The unsettling thing was that neither version of myself felt permanent and my feelings crossed over all the time. It meant that even when I was telling people I was going to take the art world by storm I could hear a little voice inside my head saying: 'I hope I'm not talking a load of bollocks here!'

Sometimes I'd take George off for a walk around the block or down to the flower market, just to clear my head and try to make sense of things. 'What the fuck have I got myself into?' I'd think. 'What if I really do become famous? I don't *want* to be famous!' George would just carry on as normal, raiding bins for discarded food and walking at my heel whenever I commanded him to. It was comforting to see him like that; not everything in my life was changing, and at least I had one constant I could rely on, my best friend George.

Around this time I got another letter from the council, and on the day it arrived I definitely felt like the old John Dolan, the stupid bastard. The letter was a demand for £800 rent arrears. Alarmingly, I had to pay the full amount within the week or I would be evicted, and I simply didn't have it.

I'd taken my eye completely off the ball when it came to paying the bills. I'd been concentrating on producing art for the show, and some days I was turning people down left, right and centre when they wanted to buy pieces from me on the High Street. By now Griff was also pushing me to produce some big, original building pieces chronicling the area, and I'd done less than half of the fifty George the Dogs and fifty High Streets I had promised to deliver.

I was sweating and panicking. I felt physically sick at the thought of being kicked out of the flat. It had been home to me and George for three years, and the prospect of homelessness at this stage in my life was unthinkable. I was in my forties now, way too old to be back on the streets, and still couldn't believe that I had got myself into such a mess at a point when my life was beginning to turn around.

Still, I didn't want to ask Griff for the £900 he was keeping for me in his office, even though that would have been the simplest thing to do. It was a matter of pride. I didn't want the embarrassment of having to explain that I was about to lose the roof over my head, and I just couldn't bring myself to go cap in hand to him, not now, especially not after everything he was doing for me.

Chapter Twenty-One

I'd proved once that I could clear my debts by selling pictures on the High Street, so I put my shoulders back and resolved to do the same again. The old me would never have had the drive to see this through, but things had changed. I was at a crossroads in my life and I had a choice: sink or swim. I knew that if I really pushed myself I could earn the money for the rent within a few days. People had been asking me if they could buy some of the large building originals I was working on for the show, and I knew I could have asked for hundreds of pounds for them. I wasn't going to flog the ones earmarked for the show, because that wouldn't have been fair to Griff, but I decided to take a break from the show work and started drawing more George the Dog and building pictures to sell to passers-by.

I hardly came up for air during the four days I sat on the freezing-cold pavement, and although it nearly killed me, I did it. I managed to raise enough money to clear my debt to the council and secure our home.

More than ever it gave me a real sense of achievement. I didn't need help: I could work my way out of a bad situation. If George had become my saviour, then it was my talent that had saved the both of us. I didn't want any wolves even turning the corner of my street, let alone at my door again. I carried on drawing, focusing on producing the show pictures, and I was grateful for every coin that passers-by put in George's cup, as that was the money that would have to keep us going for the time being.

And that's how I got to be on the street that fateful day when Griff walked up and told me that he had sold five of the collab pieces in pre-sales for a whopping £15,000. It truly was a defining moment of my life, one I'll never forget.

Of course, the money wasn't actually in the bank yet because there were invoices to be sent out, but it didn't matter to me. I wasn't desperate to get my hands on the cash; what it meant was much more important. The huge pre-sale success was proof that the hopes and dreams I'd had for these past few months were finally coming true.

I didn't tell a soul about the money except my sister Jackie, because I knew I needed to convince her to come to the show. I'm not sure she believed everything I was telling her and that was fine by me.

'This Griff, is he OK?' she asked tentatively, after I'd told her all about the pre-sales. 'Can you trust him?'

'Yes, I can, Jack. Don't worry. Just promise me you'll come to the show?'

'Alright, John, I'll do my best.'

'Promise me you'll get David and Malcolm and all their families to come too? I really want you all there.'

'I'll try, but like I said, I know they are both really busy at the moment.'

I still wasn't convinced she believed any of it. And I wouldn't have blamed her if she didn't. The next few months, leading up to the show, rolled by in an instant. I was drawing around the clock, like a machine, and every day Griff was telling me about another artist. 'OK, so far we've got Steve ESPO Powers, Zomby, Pablo Delgado, Mad C, Flying Fortress, CEPT, Gaia, C215 on board now . . .' he'd recap, remembering everyone who had agreed to contribute. I was hearing new names every day and could hardly keep up with it.

Griff had a load of books about street art in the studio, and every spare moment I had I'd be looking through them trying to learn who was who, and what they were known for. It wasn't easy; in the end we had nearly forty artists contributing.

We needed a suitable venue to host the event, and after months of searching Griff and his team got talking to the people who were renovating the building at 189 Shoreditch High Street, next to the old Leather & Suede shop. It was a beautiful twist of fate. They knew who I was, as they'd seen me every day sitting in front of the electricity box across the street, and they were more than happy to let us use the ground floor while they carried on renovating the rest of the building. They were enthusiastic about my work and one of them had even bought a picture off me.

When I'd first drawn that building three years earlier, I'd just seen it as a clapped-out old place I could use for studies, until I was good enough go up to Hampstead and draw the posh houses. If you'd told me at the time that I would have my own show inside the building, I would have said you'd lost your mind. But here I was, getting ready to hold my first ever exhibition at 189 Shoreditch High Street.

The building obviously looked quite rough and ready, as it was technically a building site, but that didn't put us off; in fact, it added to its appeal and chimed in perfectly with my image and the ethos of my work, coming from the street. Griff put up a simple sign outside saying 'Howard Griffin Gallery', and made a flyer to advertise the exhibition. The opening was set for 19 September 2013, 7.30 p.m. I could hardly wait.

Chapter Twenty-Two

We named the show 'George the Dog, John the Artist'. That was my idea; it seemed quite fitting and simple.

On one side of the flyer was Thierry Noir and ROA's collab, and on the other was a picture of me on the pavement, drawing, with George in his coat sitting in front of a paper cup wedged inside a roll of gaffer tape.

'You may not think you know John Dolan, but he is East London's most notorious artist,' the blurb read. 'Dolan sits every day with his dog George on Shoreditch High Street and documents the surrounding architecture, providing a unique insight into the changing face of contemporary Shoreditch.'

It went on to list some of the street artists who'd contributed to the collabs, and ended with the sentence 'These artists have created unique pieces by working directly onto the walls and structures of Dolan's drawn cityscapes, chronicling both the constant and the ephemeral in a city that is ever changing.'

'Fuck me,' I said when I saw it. 'He sounds great, this Dolan fella. Who is he?'

'Haven't got a clue,' George's face said. 'Sounds like a right plonker.'

Griff had done a great job, and having the flyer in my hand made it all seem very real, and very imminent. Now we needed to make sure that people came to the show. I started handing out flyers to passers-by on the High Street while I was drawing. They would stop to talk or wish me good luck, or sometimes ask me to sign their flyer. A lot of them had seen me sitting there for years, and had watched me grow as an artist.

'Will that piece you're doing now be on sale?' a few people asked. They liked the fact they could actually see me producing work for the show; my art was literally coming straight from the street.

I gave Gilbert & George a flyer one evening, when they walked past, like clockwork, at their usual time. When they walked away I shouted: 'I'd love you to come but I'll forgive you if you can't make it!'

They didn't show up, but looking back that was a blessing in disguise; they would have stolen the show.

We needed help giving out the four thousand flyers we had printed out, so I got my friend Gary Rixon on board.

He had fallen on hard times because of alcohol abuse and was also estranged from his family, and I wanted the show to help him out too. I knew Gary's father, and I phoned him up and invited him to the show, as I wanted Gary to be reunited with his loved ones, just as I hoped my family would turn up.

'I know Gary hasn't wanted to see anyone in his present condition,' I explained. 'I've been there myself and I know what it's like, but I'm gonna sort him out and take him to the show. I know he'd like to see you.'

Griff was working hard on the publicity front and managed to get a reporter from the BBC to interview me in the run-up to the show, and to film on the night.

I decided to use this as my trump card, to finally get Jackie and the rest of the family to believe what I was saying, and to come to the show.

'Listen, Jack, the show really is gonna be big,' I told her on the phone. 'And you really do have to come. The BBC are coming to interview me. I'll be on the six o'clock news.'

'Really? What day?'

'I don't know yet, but I'll let you know nearer the time.'

'Alright, you do that.'

It was frustrating, because I could tell Jackie still had her doubts. but I wasn't going to let her off the hook that easily. I didn't care if I was repeating myself or sounding desperate. I launched into a plea, to make absolutely sure I had got my message across.

'Look, Jack,' I said. 'I know I've been a complete arse-hole over the years, and I know I've let you all down, but this is my chance to finally apologise and show you I've changed. I want to feel part of the family again, rather than just being on the end of the phone.'

'I understand,' Jackie said thoughtfully. 'It's just a lot to take in. It's been a long time, John, and all this is a lot to get my head around.'

'I get that, but you have to trust me on this one, Jack. You have to be here. It's like I said before: what I want is to have my family around me again. I want you and Johnny and your girls to be there; I want Malcolm and David to come too, with their wives and kids. I know they're not kids anymore, but you know what I mean. Will you get in touch with them for me? Will you tell them what's happening and get them there? I know you can do it, Jack. I know you can talk to them.'

I could tell Jackie was worried about how this would go down, but she finally agreed to phone Malcolm and David on my behalf.

'Thanks, Jack,' I said, flooded with relief. I'd been dreaming of making it happen for such a long time, and I was relying on Jackie's support to make it work.

'Please sell it to them, Jack. Tell them it's really, really important to me, and tell them I'm sorry for being such a bastard when I was a kid, and for all the problems I've caused the family over the years. Tell them I've got my shit together now, and this is my way of apologising. I really want to gather everybody around me now, if you'll have me. I want to make you all proud.'

I couldn't have laid it on any thicker than that, and the next day Jackie put in the calls to Malcolm and David and asked them to spread the word around the extended family.

I was phoning Jackie a couple of times a week now, and every time I'd go through the same routine.

'How's David? How's Malcolm?' I'd ask. 'By the way, Jack, are they coming to the show?'

'I don't know,' she'd reply. 'To be honest with you, they really are both incredibly busy.'

I understood that Jackie couldn't make promises on their behalf and didn't want me to be disappointed, but I was determined that my nagging would pay off.

I went round to tell Les all my news, as I had been doing regularly. He'd been cooking me dinners and offering me encouragement ever since I met Griff, but during the build-up to the show his health had started to fail. He had lost so much weight he almost looked like a skeleton. I could see his life was ebbing away, even though he was only sixty-two years old.

'You show them,' he said. 'You make your family proud.' It was clear Les was already very proud of me. He'd told me recently that hearing all about the show was keeping him going. He'd supported me all the way through and vowed to hang on to see me enjoying my success on the night.

'You deserve to do well,' he said. 'I have no doubt you're going to succeed. Nothing but good will come of the show.' It was wonderful to have such unwavering support, and Les's words kept me going as the show got closer and I was working flat out to get all the drawings completed.

Seeing Les so frail and ill made me realise just how short our life can be and that if I kept on neglecting my body, it wouldn't be long before I'd end up looking the same way. I finally took the bull by the horns and got myself a prescription to get off the drugs. At long last, I held my nerve long enough to see the doctor and enrol myself in a programme to get clean. At the time, it felt as if the final piece of the puzzle had slotted into place. The short-term pain would be worth it, because I knew Les was right. Life was going to get better and better, and I didn't want anything to screw it up this time. That was what I told myself over and over again as I went through the agonies and torture of withdrawing – the cold sweats, headaches, and the terrible pain in the base of my spine and legs.

This wasn't just my future I held in my hands, it was George's too, and if I really loved him then I had to do it without compromise. I dug deep and battled through the symptoms every single day. It was the most painful thing I've been through in my life. If anyone reading this is mad enough to be thinking about taking drugs, please don't. It's a long route to suicide.

Chapter Twenty-Three

On the day of the show I began to feel incredibly apprehensive. For months I'd been the one telling Griff what a rip-roaring success it was going to be. I already had my name up in lights in Hollywood. John and George were going to be superstars and the film about my meteoric rise from the pavement to the peaks of the art world would be in cinemas within a year. My optimism and enthusiasm knew no bounds, while Griff was the one taking a much more measured and cautious view of events.

We switched roles as the hours counted down to the opening of the show, because suddenly I was the one fretting and having last-minute nerves, and Griff was being upbeat and positive and trying to reassure me.

'What if just six people turn up?' I said to Griff.

'It'll be a lot more than that, John,' he said confidently, even though he was obviously feeling the pressure too.

I kept busy that afternoon by going off to buy some new clothes.

'You don't need to be that smart,' Griff said.

'I'm not a tramp,' I told him, giving George a wink. 'I think I'm allowed to get myself some fancy new gear for the occasion.'

I could see Griff had visions of me turning up like Flash Harry, but I just got myself some new trainers and a decent fleece-lined jacket. I also bought Gary a new outfit, because I wanted him to look his best for my family.

The BBC had been filming me all week along the High Street, preparing their report to coincide with the show. One day they had me sitting under the railway bridge because it was raining, and then the reporter got me standing at the Village Underground wall under an umbrella, talking to Martin Ron, the Argentinian artist.

'We're supposed to look like we're talking about art,' I said, laughing a little nervously. 'But let's just talk any old bollocks – they'll never know.'

That's what I was saying as the camera rolled, and Martin Ron started laughing too. I was taking the piss out of the situation because it was yet more new territory for me. I felt like a fish out of water, and I needed a bit of light relief.

I was on BBC London at 6 p.m.,the night of the show. I sat with George beside me in the flat and watched it, and it made me feel really uncomfortable – much worse than when we'd been filming.

'What have I done here?' I said to George. 'I never wanted to be in the limelight like this.'

'And after that display, you'll get your wish,' said the look on his face.

During the weeks building up to the show I had also been interviewed by several local newspaper reporters, and quite a few magazine feature writers too.

I had told some of the journalists that I hadn't seen my family for the best part of twenty years, though none of their reports actually went into detail about my family background. Whenever I talked about the family reunion I was hoping for, I felt very emotional and anxious. Despite all my efforts with Jackie on the phone, I still didn't know if any of them would actually turn up.

When I finished watching the report on the TV, I started thinking about the past. So much water had passed under the bridge in the sixteen years we'd been estranged. I was twenty-five years old the last time I'd seen everyone, just days after Gerry's funeral. Would they come? I didn't have a clue. Would any bugger come? I was sweating before I even left my flat.

I knew I was going to have to give a little talk later on, and everything I wanted to say was spinning around my head. There was so much to get across. I wanted to explain how I'd tried to capture the old buildings while they were still there, because they fascinated me and Shoreditch was going through such rapid redevelopment. I wanted to talk about giving something back to society after being a prolific thief for so many years. I'd recently donated some of my work to UNICEF and the Big Issue Foundation, which raised thousands, and I was planning to do a lot more work like that. I wanted to thank all the street artists for showing me the huge amount of respect they had done by collaborating with me.

There was Gary's reunion with his dad to think about too, and that was before I even got to thanking Griff. There was so much to think about. If by some miracle my family did turn up, how was I possibly going to deal with Malcolm and David and Jackie in the midst of all this? What would it be like to have a family reunion going on at the same time as this other monumental event in my life?

Before I walked from my flat to the gallery I sat quietly on the sofa for a few minutes, trying to compose myself. George squashed himself into my side as if he was showing me how close he was to me and that he knew I needed a bit of support.

'Who am I kidding?' I thought.

There was one person I knew who definitely wouldn't be attending. Sadly, Les had passed away just a month before the show, peacefully, in his chair at home. I knew he had wanted to hang on for the show, but part of me was relieved he hadn't, because his time had come and I didn't want him to cling on and suffer on my account. 'What would Les say, eh?' I said to George as I got myself ready to leave the flat.

'This is your night,' was the answer. 'Make sure you bloody well enjoy it.'

That's exactly what Les would have said to me, and that's all I needed to know. Les had been nothing but a positive influence on me, and I was going to do him proud.

―――――――

Once I got to the gallery, I felt like a rabbit caught in the headlights. Walking up, I could see the huge queue of people lining the pavement outside. Seeing them there was surreal, because beyond them I could see my spot on the street in front of the electricity box. A guy with a flyer in his hand was standing there waiting to cross the road. It seemed so bizarre, and I couldn't take in what was happening at all. There was a massive cross-section of Shoreditch society gathering. There were hipsters next to homeless people, City boys, fashionistas, builders, students, other artists – you name it, they had all started to appear. It was like the community was pulling together for me, which is how I'd felt on the street. If people didn't buy a picture, they had put a coin in George's cup to help me sustain myself. Now they'd crossed the street with me and were still supporting me. I was very, very grateful; it was overwhelming, in fact.

When the doors opened, drinks started to flow and cameramen and photographers were pulling me in every direction. It's quite a blur in my mind now, but I remember flashbulbs were popping and journalists were waving tape recorders under my nose. The BBC World reporter Tom Donkin was there filming the show, and he interviewed me. Tom has become a friend, one of many I have made since the show, though on the night he was just one of the people who made the event feel more like a glamorous premiere than a humble art show in a dilapidated old building. 'What's all the fuss about?' I kept thinking. 'This is me, John Dolan, we're talking about!'

George appeared equally nonplussed. He looked around at everyone as if to say 'What the bleedin' hell are you lot doing here – and why are there fifty near identical drawings of me on the wall?'

The room looked amazing. Every wall was covered with my art. We had forty collaborations in total, some featuring three or four of the artists who had contributed. Five big building originals were hung at one end and had a bank of spotlights on them, and the small George the Dogs and High Streets filled an entire side wall with the collabs facing them. The repetition looked amazing.

I could see that Griff was flogging pictures left, right and centre while I talked to reporters. I tried to work my way around the room but it wasn't easy; there were two hundred people rammed inside, and another two hundred on the street outside, queuing to come in.

Unbeknownst to me, while all this was going on three taxis full of people of various ages were pulling up outside. The occupants of the taxis were all staring in astonishment at the scene before them, because they'd had their arms twisted to be here, and they were expecting a very quiet, low-key affair.

───────────

I still have to pinch myself as I write this, because I can hardly believe it's true. The people inside the taxis were Jackie and her daughters Natalie and Emily, Malcolm with his wife Gaye and their two girls Angel and Jessie, plus David and his oldest girl, Vicky, along with her husband.

They all walked in together, and every one of them looked absolutely stunned by what they were witnessing. They genuinely had thought they would be coming to a quiet space, with half a dozen people politely sipping wine. Even that would have been an achievement for me, the black sheep of the family. That's probably what they were thinking, because up until this point I had brought nothing but trouble and disappointment into their lives.

I saw Jackie and her girls first and I hugged them through a haze of emotions. I had to elbow my way through the crowds to greet all the other members of my family in turn. It was incredibly emotional to see them all after so many years, but it wasn't how you might imagine a big reunion like that to be. It was overwhelming to have them all there, right in the middle of the show, and I don't think any of us could really take it all in. When I look back now, it's like trying to recapture a dream, because it all felt so surreal. The best way I can describe it is to say that I knew it was happening, but it almost felt like it wasn't.

Malcolm and David had barely changed, and when they started to talk it felt like the years just melted away.

'What? You done all these?' Malcolm said as he looked at the collabs, which were attracting a lot of attention.

'Not quite. I'll explain it to you,' I said.

I walked him around the exhibition and told him how I met ROA and Thierry Noir and Stik, and how the domino effect kicked in with more and more street artists coming on board. Malcolm seemed genuinely impressed, and then I suddenly heard David's voice behind me. I spun around to hear him cheekily asking Griff: 'Is he robbing you, mate?'

'Shouldn't you be asking John if I'm robbing him?' Griff laughed.

I finally got to congratulate David on his MBE. I told him how I'd seen it on the news and how I was so proud of everything he had done for others in his life. I explained how because of him, I'd decided to work with charities, just like he did.

'Christie's auctioned the UNICEF one and raised thousands,' I said. 'I'm proud of that. I want to do more stuff like that.'

He grinned and said: 'You should be proud. That's what it's all about, my son.'

I honestly could have cried. I had wanted to make my family proud for so many years, and had all but given up hope such a short time ago. Now I could scarcely believe I'd finally done it – and in such a spectacular way.

When the time came for me to stand up and say a few words, people crowded onto the old staircase along the back of the gallery to get a vantage point. The room fell silent, and I felt everybody's eyes on me as I began to talk. George was by my side, cool and collected like he always has been.

I started explaining the concept of the collaborations and I think I said something about how I hoped my pictures of the street would open up people's eyes to the world around them.

As I spoke, I made eye contact with Jackie's oldest girl, Natalie. She's a beautiful young woman now and I hadn't seen her since she was very small. Seeing her standing there filled me with so much joy and nearly brought me to tears. I had to bite my lip to carry on. When I spotted David's daughter Vicky, she had the same effect on me. I hadn't seen her since she was a young teenager, and now she's a successful accountant.

'I'll have to have a chat with you about your tax,' she smiled when we chatted afterwards. It was amazing to see all of the kids – all my nieces and nephews – as accomplished adults.

Gary's dad came along and, although I didn't get to spend much time with them, I know they had their reunion after many years apart. That meant a great deal to me, because I wanted my art to do so much more than just make a few quid for me and George. As David had said when I told him about my charity work, 'That's what it's all about.' This night was life-changing for me, and I wanted to use that change in a positive way, to help others.

A dear old friend of mine, Georgie Tricks, came along too, which also made my night. He's one of the mates I broke into a car mechanic's yard with when I was fourteen. He had his son with him, who has learning difficulties, and it brought a lump to my throat to meet him for the first time, and to see Georgie again after twenty-odd years. In fact, I was so moved I asked if there was anything I could do for his son. I'd have given him the money for a trip to Disneyland or anything, I felt so emotional about seeing him. Georgie told me his son wasn't allowed to fly, but he still appreciated the offer. Georgie didn't actually need any help from me or anybody else, as he had done very well for himself, marrying his childhood sweetheart, Tracy, and working in a good job for an advertising agency. I was absolutely delighted for him, and I knew Dot would have been too. She had been best friends with Georgie's mum, Annie, and the two mothers used to worry themselves silly about what would become of the pair of us. I think both Dot and Annie would have been amazed and very proud at how Georgie and I had turned out in the end.

As the night wore on I went outside to get a breath of fresh air, because I was starting to feel a bit over overwrought. There were so many people standing shoulder to shoulder and I was boiling hot, not to mention emotionally strung out with my past and present lives colliding like this.

'You alright?' Georgie asked me, because he'd gone outside for a breath of air too.

'I think I'm in shock,' I found myself saying. 'I feel like a stranger in a strange land.'

I'm not sure Georgie knew what to say to that, but he didn't have to reply, because suddenly a woman's voice cut in, saying: 'John, d'you remember me?'

'Course I do,' I said as soon as I looked up and saw her face. 'You're Sarah!'

I hadn't seen her since she was a teenager but I recognised her straight away: Sarah was Jimmy Dolan's oldest girl.

'We saw you on the news,' she started to explain. 'Dad's been wondering where you've been all these years.'

I asked after Jimmy, of course, and Sarah told me he had had a leg amputated, on account of his diabetes. I was very sorry to hear that, and I told her to stay in touch. I wanted to ask her if Jimmy had tried looking for me, but I didn't. There were a hundred questions I wanted to ask, but I was reaching the point where I couldn't take any more in. These were conversations to have in the future; I could only deal with so much in one night.

By 10 p.m. I couldn't wait to go home. My nerves were frayed, and I felt physically and emotionally exhausted. I needed to just be alone with George, to try to take in everything that had happened.

It wasn't until the following day that I learned how much we'd sold and I started to really appreciate the significance of the day.

All the George the Dogs and High Street buildings had gone for between £20 and £50 each on the night and we'd sold 30 collabs off the walls, ranging in price from £500 to £3,500. Total sales amounted to £35,000, which meant, with the £15,000 from pre-sales, we'd flogged fifty grand's worth of art, all told.

Fifty big ones! It didn't seem real, but the money wasn't nearly as important as what had happened with my family.

'When I pulled up in the cab and saw so many people at the show, it made me so proud,' David had told me. It was an incredible moment in my life when he said that; he could not have said anything better. I'd been the bane of my family's life for decades, but I'd finally come good. To have that acknowledged by my big brother meant absolutely everything to me. I could have died and gone to heaven at that point, because I'd achieved my lifelong ambition.

'I told you I was gonna make it, didn't I?' I said to George eventually, because he was watching me very closely while I was deep in thought, processing all these life-changing events in my head.

'I've made my family proud, and we've made fifty big ones!' I said, giving him a pat. 'Who'd have thought it?'

George now had the same wry look on his face he'd had on the day Griff told me about the pre-sales, the one that said 'When do I get my half?'

I scooped him in my arms and gave him a bloody big hug. He deserved more than half. I owed George absolutely everything.

Epilogue

The process of writing my book has made me ask two huge questions. Where did it all go wrong . . . and where did it all go right?

Eight months have now passed since the exhibition, and I am still taking in what a seismic change my life has gone through.

As I've said before, I didn't just see the show as a way of making money and securing the future for myself and George. I wanted it to make a difference to other people's lives too, by inspiring other homeless people and hopefully anybody else out there who is experiencing similar problems to the ones I went through.

Being offered the chance to write this book was a real gift, because it's given me the opportunity to share the details of my past and explain how and why I went off the rails. I sincerely hope that anybody reading this who is lucky enough to have had a better start in life than me will appreciate how shit happens to some people, because that's just the way it is.

————————

I wasn't born bad. I didn't have genes that automatically made me into a burglar, a drug addict or a homeless person. I was simply dealt a bad hand in life, like so many other people in the world, and it took me a long time to shuffle the pack and finally put my house in order.

I don't blame anybody. Plenty of people have a far worse start than me, and I have learned that whatever cards you are dealt, life is ultimately what you make it. You have to look for your talents – because we all have them – and you have to use the skills you have to dig yourself out of the shit as best you can, time and time again if necessary.

When I look back, I can't believe I had the audacity, or the bollocks, to carry out so many burglaries over so many years. I am certainly not proud of my criminal past in any way, even if the memories of some of the scrapes I got into still make me laugh out loud today.

In my younger days I tried to kid myself that the type of crime I specialised in didn't harm anybody, but I don't see it like that now. No crime is victimless, even if you're knocking off a frigging Dunkin' Donuts shop!

————————

When Griff and I were putting the show together I kept saying to him that we had to be charitable, because I truly believe that what goes around comes around. I was on the receiving end of a lot of charity myself when I was on the street, and I desperately wanted to start giving something back to society.

The charitable work I've done so far, for UNICEF and the Big Issue Foundation, is just the start. I have also helped Centrepoint by providing artwork for a charity auction, and I've recently taken part in a community-based art project with the Museum of London. My ambition is to support global charities and help people in India who don't even have access to basic medical care or drinking water, let alone a roof over their head.

Following the success of my exhibition, Griff established the Howard Griffin gallery as a permanent space at 189 Shoreditch High Street. And at the end of this year Griff and I are putting on an exhibition in LA, similar to my London show, but using an LA landscape as the basis for new collaborations. I honestly can't believe it – it's fucking unreal! It still feels like a miracle to me that I've even got a passport and the money to get to the USA, let alone to be putting on an art exhibition there.

My sister Jackie turned fifty earlier this year, and I was invited to her party, in a smart venue on Chancery Lane.

'You're coming, ain't ya?' Malcolm said to me beforehand.

'Who'll be there?' I asked.

'Family and friends,' he said. 'You've got to be there!'

The conversation was one I could only have dreamed of having such a short time before, and of course I went along.

Jackie looked really well and was surrounded not just by the family, but lots of people from her past, like old school pals and friends I knew from President House.

Just like at the show, it was a lot to take in. Many people knew about the problems I'd had over the years and I felt a bit edgy, to be honest, worrying about what they might be saying about me. They could have been saying good things now, of course, but I wasn't sure.

I didn't stay late, and I made my excuses and left. This isn't a Hollywood, bubblegum version of my life, and I don't want to pretend there is a perfect, happy-ever-after ending, because it's not true. In reality, it is going to take time for me to rebuild all the bridges I've broken over the years, but I am just so grateful to have the chance, and I am not going to blow it. I have finally learned my lessons.

———————

George was asleep when I got home that evening and I sat looking at him for a long time, thinking about what might have happened had he not walked into my life.

It blew my mind completely. How could a Staffie have changed my life like he had? It was absolutely mental, but totally and utterly true.

I really do owe George a tremendous debt, and I hope he knows how much I love him.

ACKNOWLEDGMENTS

With thanks to all the artists from around the world who have done me the great honour of collaborating with me; I am extremely grateful to you all.

2501 (Italy)

Agostino Iacurci (Italy)

Ben Wilson (aka Chewing Gum Man) (UK)

Broken Fingaz Crew (Israel)

BRK (Spain)

C215 (France)

CEPT (UK)

Christiaan Nagel (South Africa)

Cityzen Kane (UK)

David Walker (UK)

Dscreet (Australia)

Ekta (Sweden)

Flying Fortress (Germany)

Gold Peg (UK)

Gaia (USA)

Hitnes (Italy)

Ian Stevenson (UK)

Kid Acne (UK)

Know Hope (Israel)

Liqen (Spain)

MadC (Germany)

Malarky (UK)

Martin Ron (Argentina)

Maser (Ireland)

Michael De Feo (USA)

Pablo Delgado (Mexico)

Pelucas (Spain)

Pez (Spain)

ROA (Belgium)

Ronzo (Germany)

Rowdy (UK)

RUN (Italy)

Sever (USA)

Steve ESPO Powers (USA)

Stik (UK)

Swet (Denmark)

The London Police (UK)

The Rolling People (UK/Spain)

Thierry Noir (France)

Zomby (UK)

In addition to the artists, many people pulled together to help me on this journey and without them all it would not have been possible for George and me.

Thanks once more to all of the artists who did me the honour to collaborate with me. Thank you David Burns for letting me use his office rooftop to draw the Shoreditch skyline from and thanks to Carina Claassens for making sure I actually got up there. A special thanks to Ron and Oren Rosenblum for so generously donating 189 Shoreditch High Street for my exhibition. An extra special thank you to Hannah Zafiropoulos for her relentless hard work and organisational skills and also for searching the streets of Shoreditch for the right location for the show. Thanks to Dave and Paddy Evans and Robin Phillips for all of their help on the opening day hanging all of the works; without them there would have been nothing on the walls. Thanks to Gary Rixon for handing out the show flyers all around Shoreditch. Thanks to Will Robson-Scott, Marcus Peel, Albert Thorne, Rob Weir and Tom Donkin for their skills behind the camera. Thanks to Silja Andersen from *The Big Issue* Foundation and to Francesca Giorgi-Monfort and David Morris for their help and patience. Thanks to everyone who came to the opening of the show and helped make it one of the most enjoyable nights of my life, and a further thanks to all those who bought a piece of my artwork on the night.

Thanks to my editor Jack Fogg at Random House and the whole team there who worked hard to make this book happen. Thanks as well to Rachel Murphy for all of her help and support.

A heartfelt thank you from George and me to the community of Shoreditch who supported us for three years on the High Street. When they weren't buying drawings, they were putting money in George's cup and when they weren't doing that, people would always offer words of encouragement.

Thanks to Big Ben and Paul at the Rainbow Sports Bar who always watched my back on a Friday night when all the crazy drunks were out partying in Shoreditch.

And lastly thanks to Richard Howard-Griffin, aka Griff. Without his friendship and dedication none of this could have happened.

Picture Acknowledgements

Photographs

All images pages 4 and 5, bottom of page 8 © Albert Julià Torné

All images pages 6 and 16, bottom of page 15 © Rob Weir

All other images courtesy of the author or Richard Howard-Griffin.

Every reasonable effort has been made to contact all copyright holders, but if there are any errors or omissions, we will insert the appropriate acknowledgement in subsequent printings of the book.

All illustrations © John Dolan

And as the sun went down and the day came to an end,
John Dolan the artist and George the dog lived happily ever after.